Life in the Hotel

Life in the Hotel

Hotel History

Jo Jean Thomas DeHony

To order additional copies of this book, contact:
Xlibris LLC
1-888-795-4274
www.Xlibris.com
Orders@Xlibris.com
551396

CONTENTS

DEDICATION

DEDICATED TO MY Mother Erma J. Thomas who helped me through all of the remodeling, the guests, maid work, new endeavors that we would start, good and bad, thick and thin, the laughter and tears we had many times during the hours of hard labor and to all of many different and strange happenings.

My father Cal Thomas, who taught me imagination, determination, and to give a lot of thought to try anything I wanted to tackle.

My family and friends who were always there when I needed them. The staff I had to rely on for daily operation. The guest that returned year after year, and the businesses that were available when I needed repairs, and when I needed to purchase the items that helped with the success of the Hotel.

32 years of owning a small hotel in the middle of down town Cody, a Tourist town, provided me with many opportunities, changes, mysteries, a never ending supply of friends. Getting into the lives of people in need of help, the people that were thankful for what they had, and even the people that did not appreciate anyone or anything that was available to them.

PREFACE

WHEN I FIRST started thinking about a book, or books describing the Hotel, the past, the present, I thought it would be volumes, rather than a book. There have been so many thing that have happened from the conception continuing through the years of the development of Cody, all of the buildings, the people, right through the changes of ownership of the Hotel, from Chamberlin Boarding House, Hotel Chamberlin, Pawnee Hotel, and through the date of the sale in 2005, now called the Chamberlin Inn.

I knew when I first started writing in 1982 there was a story, but for some reason I stopped, and could not go any further. Then in 2012, I could not resist the temptation of trying again. This was after I had been given editorials and complete writings by Agnes Chamberlin. Many pictures were given to me, along with finding items in the small wooden box in the attic, many articles, the menu from the Irma for their grand opening, old small flags, Mrs Chamberlin's dance cards, and a great deal of information that took me back to the time when the Hotel Chamberlin was first being build and opened for business. I wanted to describe in detail the information that I felt was worth sharing with others. Much of this information came from the old original hotel registers, which were given to me by the previous owners. The way the hotel developed over the years, along with all of the things I could remember happening while I owned the hotel. I would type and work on it for several evenings and then in no time I would remember another incident. Every time I sit down. I would think, "how can this be put on paper", there have been so many days with so many guests and changes I would never reach completion.

I believe the only way it will ever be published is try to find a spot to end. I know in my mind that there have been enough eventful happenings' during my ownership of the hotel, that I have not changed my thoughts, and views, through all of the chaos, excitement and good times. I believe it will be even more interesting and enlightening to the readers. Therefore, I want to take them on a journey through the years, of building a life—long business as well as the involvement into several lives. A Hotel that is still standing and is being revived, by new ownership. Hopefully, they will enjoy many future years of interesting and exciting happenings.

Jo Jean Thomas DeHony
2013

CHAMBERLIN BOARDING HOUSE
HOTEL CHAMBERLIN
PAWNEE HOTEL
CHAMBERLIN INN
CODY, WYOMING
1897 THROUGH 2005

CHAPTER 1

LIFE IN THE HOTEL

L IFE IN THE HOTEL, IS ONLY A PART OF THE HISTORY IN THIS BOOK

NAMES OF GUESTS OR SUBJECTS OF PARTICULAR STORIES WILL BE WITHHELD AND OR CHANGED FOR PROTECTION OF IDENTITY.

I am not a writer, but I do hope that I have put together a book that will be interesting to my readers and lead you into over 100 years of starting a small business, that is still very much alive.

Created by hard work, determination and imagination that brought individual success.

"Owning a hotel started with my desire to own a beauty shop"

Being employed by HUSKY OIL COMPANY and had worked from a clerk typist to an Executive Secretary, and at that time decided I needed to start my own business. This was discussed with the full approval from my boss, who was an Executive Vice President and who immediately encouraged me to do whatever I wanted.

I have inserted a time line at this place in the book, to help you follow the Hotel History.

With so many changes, and work on the hotel made it necessary for me to do in-depth search on the time line of the Chamberlin. This time line was corrected and updated on March 2004, and again in 2013 to make certain the dates and information was correct

CHAPTER 2

TIME LINE

1871	January 20, Agnes Brown (Chamberlin) born New Milford, Illinois.
1897	Agnes spent five months in Wheatland, Wyoming, working for I. O. Middaugh, editor of Newspaper, *The Wheatland World.*
1897	Enrolled in commercial college in Wichita, Kansas.
1898	Agnes met Mark in Woodward, Oklahoma
1899	February 6, Agnes and Mark married in Peabody, Kansas
1900	Mark practices dentistry in Hartville, Wyoming
1900	March 17, Agnes joins Mark in Hartville. They leave Hartville.
1900	Begin covered wagon trip north through Wyoming, ending in Cody August 26th.
1900	Buy a lot from George T. Beck in 1200 Block of Main Street. Gus Holm and father build One room house with lumber from Hud Darrah's sawmill, they also built a "barn October 18, 1900"
1901	Agnes works as a typesetter for the Cody Enterprise across the street from her future hotel on 2nd Street, (now 12th Street).
1902	Mark, Agnes, and Dewey take a wagon hunting trip to Towgotee Pass area, going via Sunlight, Cooke City, YNP, Moran, then return via Dubois, hit Red Lodge-Meeteetse Trail back to Cody.
1903	February 10, bought Lot 11, Block 50
1903	Take better equipped trip to YNP over new road via North Fork and Sylvan Pass.
1904	That spring move from Main Street around the corner to 12th street to Block 50. Hud Darrah again traded lumber for dental work and they borrowed money and built their first white frame boarding house on Lot 11, Block 50.
1904	May 27, bought Lot 10, Block 50

1904	Dr. Chamberlin went to Chicago (?) and got a $50 dental diploma. He built a brick office North, and adjacent to hotel. Documented in the City of Cody's minutes of Council meeting.
1905	Agnes started "boarding house" with two tables full.
1906	Agnes and her sister Bertha inherited $5,000 each.
1906	Photo of Hotel Chamberlin in *Wyoming Industrial Journal*. Article mentions dental office.
1906	Flour Mill investment
1908	Flour Mill closes (reopens briefly years later)
1909	Clipping from Agnes' Scrapbook "September 25, Dr Chamberlin built a "20 x 20" brick office on a lot to the north of his present location". BECOMES THE FIRST COURT HOUSE.
1909	Mark makes application to City to build a brick and stone building on Lot 6 in Block 50.
1910	Mable Watson comes to work and Agnes starts "serving meals".
1909 or 1910	Mark bought relinquishment on place up Trail Creek.
1912	Bertha Brown, Agnes' sister marries and moves away. She had been with her since 1903.
1916	Sold farm east of Cody.
1917	March 28th started building new hotel.
1918	Agnes added more rooms for $8000. Moved old barn around and made it into ANNEX.
1918	Dining room could seat 25 at 5 tables.
1920	Closed Dining room and turned space into "several bedrooms. Paid off all of her debts. Inherited $3,000, bought an $1800 Oldsmobile to replace the Saxon.
1922	Mark died August 17 in the Powell Hospital.
1926	Agnes hosts the first meeting the Buffalo Bill Museum at the hotel. She is elected the first President. Agnes became very busy in Cody, she was the founder of the Christian Science Church, Cody Music Club, Cody's Women's Club, Play-readers, Eastern Star, Pioneers of Cody Country.
1932	Addition added to top of dental office.
1935	Agnes gave her "homestead land" to City of Cody so airport could be enlarged.
1939	Sold to Hattie and George Edwards. Edwards owned for 37 years.
1939	Agnes retired to stucco house on the corner of 10th and Cody Avenue.

1940	Agnes writes The Story of Cody Club.
1941	Hattie and George Edwards changed name to Pawnee Hotel. Not sure about the exact date but the Pawnee Hotel was Operated by Avis O'Neill and her husband
1947	Agnes helps dedicate Cody's first radio station KODI
1949	Agnes B. Chamberlin died January 17th at the age of 78. Mayor Hugh Smith orders all Cody businesses to close for the day so that all might attend her funeral.
	Pawnee Hotel was being operated by Ray and Winnie Skelton for a short time and again, not certain of the date.
1974	Jo Jean DeHony purchases the Pawnee Hotel, while still working for Husky Oil Company. She started remodeling immediately and operated the hotel for nearly 32 years. During this time Jo Jean purchased and ran an Insurance Agency, along with raising, training and selling Tennessee Walkers. Pawnee Hotel went through name changes from the Pawnee Hotel, Pawnee Lodge, and before being sold was again named the Pawnee Hotel.
2005	Pawnee Hotel sold in October to Ev and Susan Diehl.
	The Hotel again went through a name change to CHAMBERLIN INN, and has under gone many remodeling changes.

CHAPTER 3

REASONS FOR PURCHASING OLD HOTEL

THE RESULT OF buying an old Hotel, started in 1974 when I decided I wanted a beauty shop. It started with many days and weeks of dealing with an owner of a large hotel on main street, and ended with not being able to agree on the contract terms, so I jumped in the car, drove across the street, down a half block and stopped in front of the Pawnee Hotel, at 1032 12th street, a red brick hotel built around 1900 and in need of a face lifting. The rooms were badly in need of interior remodeling. The yard was filled with weeds and not the best looking building in down town Cody. I could see it was not going anywhere. I noticed a very old hotel that was in disrepair, along with tumbleweeds, and rag weeds so plentiful that you could not see the apartment building to the east of the lot that set on 12th and Rumsey Street.

The old Hotel had a very old neon sign that illuminated HOTEL in large letters and in very small letters was Pawnee. I made a sharp right turn, into the curb, slammed on the breaks and found I was immediately in front of the brick building with badly worn windows, that needed painted, and repaired, but had character that called to me for help.

I jumped out of my car and ran up the cement steps into an old wooden door that was actually beautiful with the beveled glass in each pane. I would guess the door to have approximately 15 individual windows. I ran into the second lobby, as I passed through a small entrance between 2 doors. I was greeted by a large elderly lady at the desk in the front lobby, she asked "what I wanted"? I asked her, "is this place for sale" she replied "yes", much to my surprise, and we then discussed the price somewhat, and I left. I really became intrigued and decided I would check into it further.

I thought about our conversation and it came to mind I felt it was not the right thing. Something was wrong? What could it be? The next day I checked at the court house and found who owned this property. It was owned by the Edwards family in Cody. The owner of this property was one of the sons of the family. The Edwards family owned several properties in Cody.

Finding the owners lived in Billings, Montana. I drove to Billings the next week, met with the owner, visited with him for a while, and after a long discussion, the owner gave me a price. I in turn made an offer, and it was rejected with the agreement that he would advertise the property for sale. If it did not sell in that time they would visit with me and sell the hotel to me for my offer. I was nervous, excited, and scared all at the same time. And that is really a strange way to feel, but I did.

I, as you can imagine, really hoped with all my heart that it would not sell and I could buy it. If that happened I needed to get real busy and visit with my boss, the bank, and everyone involved to make sure I was ready. One month later he called. Mr. Edwards could not sell the building or the property, so we then agreed on terms, a contract was completed and behold, the whole thing started. I was to meet the owner at midnight in front of the Pawnee Hotel to sign papers, get the keys, and become the new owner of the Hotel and property. I entered the hotel to wait for the owner and visit with the lady that has been renting the Hotel, but when we came face to face, she realized she had set herself up for a fall. She had really tried to bilk me out of my money, and to sell what did not belong to her. She literally chased me out of the Hotel Lobby with a screwdriver in her hand. I was truly afraid she might stab me in the back, as I turned and very slowly but with a swift step exited through the front door. I made it to my vehicle and sit in it still shaking while I waited for the real owner to get there. When he arrived he asked me "why are you outside", I told him "she scared me", so he bravely walked into the lobby. He had just told me they had always had a good repore. It was not a minute until he came out in a blaze, and said "I think she is crazy". With that happening we both stayed outdoors until exactly 12: midnight, the hour we were to close on the purchase of the property, and I would take over the ownership. We walked in, got the keys, and made the final transaction. She was gone. (The lady that had been renting the hotel from the owner)

I owned a hotel " I DID". I PURCHASED ME A HOTEL, In June of 1974. What an exciting and great experience for me to fall into. I had never worked in a hotel, much less been an owner or involved with the hotel business in any way.

On July 1, 1974 the Pawnee Hotel was purchased by Jo Jean DeHony, a single woman of about 34, little did she know what she had to look forward to, and little did she know the pleasure, upset, laughter, and disasters that would befall her in the future years.

JO JEAN THOMAS DEHONY

CHAPTER 4

TIME TO START REMODELING

WHEN WE COMPLETED the transaction, I was really shocked at seeing the inside of the Hotel. This lady had made a bare disaster of the hotel prior to my taking possession. It looked like a skeleton stripped of all it's flesh. It left a very devastated looking building.

She had ripped all of the rubber back carpet up, and did not scrape the pieces of rubber off the floor. The wall paper was coming off the walls, and I was not sure if I would ever get it fixed up to look like what I had thought I would like it to be.

All furnishings, all bedding was gone, and she had sold the check in counter which was located in the front lobby, used for the registration desk. The huge clothes dryer that was hooked up to the gas line, as well as the washing machine both operated in the basement, were gone. Everything that could be removed, down to the plug and switch plates, not to mention many light fixtures, and any item that would make it possible for me to start operating the hotel was gone. It was in a terrible state of needing repair and furnishings. I decided, now is the time to start from scratch.

I got in touch with furniture stores, carpet houses, hotel linen suppliers, and figured out how I could make a desk that would work in the front lobby until I could come up with what I wanted as permanent furnishings. This started my preparing for a new face lift.

I purchased all new carpets, new beds, new sinks, new showers, a lot of paneling, ceiling tile, televisions, and anything you could think that would be needed in order to remodel and get ready for business. The wiring in the building was completely redone, and much of the plumbing was redone. This went on for a year, but I had one job to finish in a hurry . . . I had a contract with the railroad and needed to get the railroaders back into the hotel as soon as possible, so by September, I completed 5 very nice rooms and they were able to move back in. Each room then had their own shower. They no longer had to use the share shower in the hall. They had new beds, with firm mattresses, and wood headboards, beautiful dressers, new carpet and drapes, and the only thing missing for a month was a lobby. I had an old switchboard, (cord board) and that was used for the desk and the phone, but it didn't take long for me to construct a counter, and make the lobby look inviting and ready for business.

I then proceeded to deal with the guest, and found that was never anything more interesting than an old hotel. This started with its past, and character.

The first customer I had after the rail roaders, was a sheepherder that had been herding sheep for months and came to Cody for a night on the town. The room I had ready was #6, a very nice room with bright lavender walls, and a lovely bathroom, with a large old fashion tub, also painted lavender and had large gold cherebs or cupid decals floating around on the body of the outside of the tub. I charged him $12.00 for the nights lodging. After he had cleaned up he came to the front lobby and was so pleased and marveled about the nice room. He made it through the night and we saw him many times after that, always wanting the same room.

I had purchased a hotel on a Secretary salary, and then I wondered how I would pay for it, but at the time of the purchase the Burlington Northern Railroad housed two crews in the hotel every night, and I had it figured I would be able to have that check make my payments, and the utilities. I truly prayed it would work out and I could operate the hotel until I could get the beauty shop ready. Remember! It was the main reason I purchased this beautiful old building.

A lot of things were happening at the same time. I also purchased the house I had been renting, as the owners made me an offer I could not turn down. Everything was falling into place at one time and I was truly scared and shaking to think of what I was doing.

As soon as I had signed the papers, started the moving process, and getting ready for the renovation I had one person after another stopping by and asking what I planned to do with the Old Pawnee. I had many of the old timers come into the hotel afraid I was going to tear it down and tell me of all the happenings over the years. They were also afraid I would change the name, and at that time the first thing I did was assure them that I would do neither, but instead, remodel and run it as the beautiful old hotel it really was and at this time still is.

They each had their idea of what I should do, or their tale as to what they heard I would be doing. Many very interesting stories and I listened intently. One of those may just be the answer and work out.

We will now continue with the adventure of the remodeling and operations of the Pawnee Hotel.

I had a few couples, or single people that stopped by to look at the hotel and relate their story to me of how they had stayed in the hotel on their wedding night, or eaten dinner on a special occasion, which was served by Mrs. Chamberlin or her Sunday Dinner, which consisted of fried chicken. The special dinners were served in a very large room next to the kitchen with a number of neatly set up individual tables, arranged especially for her guest. I was ask not to tear down the building, and each person had their own questions and wondered if it would be a place for elderly, or a special gift shop, or if it would become a nice restaurant. With each idea, and suggestion, I would tell them, "that sounds like a good idea, and I will give that some thought". And that is exactly what I did. I gave thoughts to the many ideas many times.

The abundance of stories I was told about the Chamberlin, or the Pawnee Hotel, made it so interesting, and filled me with enthusiasm, which only gave me another good reason for my purchasing this property.

I had to move the railroaders out while I was getting some rooms remodeled, and filled with beds, furnishings and carpet. I proceeded immediately working all day at the Oil Company, and all night trying to remodel the hotel. As soon as I had five rooms ready it was time to get the railroaders back in the hotel and make some money for my first payment. I then remodeled rooms as they came up and the first room I had ready for rent was a room in the back of the hotel that had been the previous operator's bedroom.

There was a lot of time spent in the remodeling, moving beds, and for two months I had mattresses and box springs stacked in the front lobby, almost to the ceiling. As a room was finished they would be moved into that room, with the help of several people, but the most of the moving with assisted by a very able guest, a nice looking man from Illinois that had been a cop there and came to Wyoming for a vacation. In order for him to have a room to sleep in he had to help me move the bed into that room, and with him staying at the hotel for several weeks, he was invited to help with moving beds into the rooms on several occasions. This became a good laugh over the years, as each time he returned to Cody for vacation he would arrive about the time I was changing out a room and guess what? That's right! Moving beds and he helped!

picture by Jo Jean DeHony

Welcome traveler

With locally purchased furnishings, this newly decorated room in the Pawnee awaits visitors. Remodeling work continues as Jo Jean Dehoney whips the old building into shape.

"The Pawnee was the headquarters for the Yellowstone Park Bus Lines."

Story b

I had purchased enough furniture to outfit the hotel for business, and was trying all the time to get beauty supply equipment, but needed a place to store these items until I could use them, as the hotel was being torn up and put back together as time would permit. It left very little space for storage of anything except beds, mattresses, dressers, TV's, chairs and decor for the rooms that were being remodeled. This also included new plumbing, new sinks, showers and toilet stools, not to mention all of the fixtures and decoration needed to make it all fall into place.

A good friend of mine had purchased the old Safeway building on 12th and Beck, and offered that space to me until he was able to lease it out to some business. I appreciated his offer, and took him up on it.

JO JEAN THOMAS DEHONY

CHAPTER 5

INTERESTING DISCOVERIES

I T WAS NOT just getting the rooms ready, but ripping out the walls to redo the electrical, which we found it had been redone at least 5 times, with the different types of wire and connections they used as well as the plumbing, and the sewer lines, which took many hours we found when we were redoing the electrical that nice old hotel was build to stand, and had 2 x 12 boards stacked 5 deep for fire walls. The lath and plaster adorned the walls, the ceilings, and brick walls, which zoomed up every time we decided to tear out a wall. While feeding electrical wiring and plumbing in walls with the 2 x 12 being so thick it took a lot of drilling and tearing out plaster. That is when I decided the only thing I could do, since I did not know how to plaster, I decided the hotel would be paneled in all halls, and rooms with the paneling I chose that would make each room different and add a new face lift to the beautiful old building that had been build with much care and love. I soon noticed all the brick walls I found through-out the hotel gave me more input into the building of the original hotel had been build onto on all sides, back, front, and then starting on the second story found it to be a very fire safe and well built building, I also found a large steel fire door in the basement dividing the rooms from the furnace, or the old boiler room. This was a fire safety measure. On the South west end of the basement near the boiler was a large room with a plain wooden door, secured closed with a small metal latch, and this very room is where I found some very nice glass panel doors in a beautiful walnut color that were so black you did not know they were there. This led to a great discovery in my finding a large coal opening from the alley into the down stairs window, for the purpose of unloading the coal into the room next to the boiler. I rescued the doors only to find they belonged on the front glassed in lobby upstairs, just in front of the main lobby which had been chosen as the place for checking in guest. They were cleaned up, polished, and installed into the door openings where they had been originally placed many years ago. A part of the hotel was gaining the original structure.

In the front of the Hotel, the basement windows opened onto the sidewalk, this was not acceptable to the more modern streets and sidewalks. I immediately cemented them in and this eliminated the basement windows from all future opening and use. This was on the West side of the basement. We then went around to the North side of the hotel and sealed off the windows to the basement and at that time when I put in a new sidewalk.

Step saving device

This laundry chute ends in the basement of the Pawnee and was used in the original building to save steps for maids. A laundry closet on the second floor contains a drop for laundry. Soiled linens dropped two floors to be laundered.

picture by Jo Jean DeHony

Another great discovery was in the basement where the laundry had been done. The dirty laundry was passed down the laundry chutes from upstairs to main floor and down into the basement, where the ladies did the laundry and folding then placed the clean linens in a dumb-waiter to be lifted or carried upstairs to be placed in the laundry closets for the next day usage.

picture by Jo Jean DeHony

1917 era water closet located in the basement of Hotel Chamberlin. This ancient water closet remains in the basement of the Pawnee. **It** is still in working order.

The most fascinating item I had discovered in the basement of the hotel was a BRASS TOILET. This amazing piece of plumbing was made on the same concept of the flushing as the new modern toilets at the airport in the late 90's. This toilet worked in this way: when you put the lid down the toilet filled with water from a large galvanized tank that hung from the wall and was plumbed to the cold water. After use and you stood up, the lid on the stool came up, it would flush the stool. What an invention, and it was installed in the early 1900's.

Near the furnace, on the wall that went upstairs from the basement to the alley, and the crawl space under the entire back of the hotel, was located the panel and the wiring for the original phone system.

Picture by Jo Jean DeHony

The system that was still there at the time I purchased the hotel, which was an old cord switchboard with the red and white lights that indicated rings, if a room was connected, if it was an incoming or outgoing call, and the handle cranked in order to ring out. The rooms would be connected, and you would push a button to ring them. At that time all lines were open and you could listen in on calls if it was necessary. I guess that was how a lot of news was transferred in those days.

The cord switchboard is not an easy phone to learn so I but in a more modern unit that was a very nice switchboard, approximately 24 inches wide, slanting back at approximately 16 inches from the front to back with 16 individual phone extensions. You would just pull a lever down to ring and up to hook up the room. That system worked for several years, but as time went on I replaced the system with a very small unit, and very modern approximately 6 inches wide and 10 inches from front to back. This new and very modern phone system was complete with the latest of everything from wake up call, transfer calls, connect rooms, and it made the entire communication for the hotel very easy and even brought us up to using credit card machines, music while you waited for the calls to go through. This made a very small and nice looking telephone system. (Still using the old wires brittle, and very dainty, but worked as well in the 90's as they did 50 years before, and they were still attached and connected to the phone box in the basement). They worked great. Every room had a telephone, a wake-up call rather than the alarm clocks, privacy. No more news over the phone lines.

Everyday and most every minute from the time I purchased the hotel there was changes and something happening, some good and some bad, but never a dull moment.

A lot of fixing, a lot of making it better, a lot of excitement and a lot of short nights with very little sleep. I was getting more and more check-ins' from 3 P.M. and all night. I soon became so used to this that I would jump up check in a customer, and head back to bed, fall asleep immediately and get rest until the next time the door bell rang.

There were times I wondered, and became frustrated as there was always a water break, a drain line springing a leak in the old orange burg, and this usually happened in the middle of the night. These leaks were in pipes that had yet to be fixed. There were a lot of showers that ran over, as people just didn't understand the curtains kept the water in the base of the shower and sent it down the drain. I truly had a lot of water damage in the hotel, as you will read about as we go on with the enjoyment of owning a hotel, and even more the enjoyment of owning a very old hotel.

Soon I had more interested persons coming by and reminiscing. They told me of the times they worked in the basement in the laundry, or when they were a little girl they had helped their aunt in the dining room sitting up the tables, and getting the dining room ready for guest. These stories enhanced my joy of owning the Pawnee as they brought back many hours of the past.

One of the exciting things when I was first remodeling the hotel, I had a young man working for me and working on the room upstairs. The law came after him and was going to arrest him. I asked them if they would wait until noon and he would come off the roof for lunch. They were going to go after him and use force if necessary. I was afraid he would jump off the roof and maybe take one of the other guys with him. I insisted they wait, and they did. When he came out for lunch they arrested him and it all happened with very little incident.

A great mystery, and I never truly found anything out about it. I had a HOLE IN BASEMENT FLOOR, and when you looked into the hole through the cement, you could only see darkness, even with a flashlight you could see only darkness, SO I KEPT IT A BIG MYSTERY.

THE PAWNEE HOTEL IT WAS SURROUNDED BY BARS, A LIQUOR ESTABLISHMENT, EAGLE CLUB, VETS CLUB, WONDER BAR, BUFFALO BILL BAR, SMITH LIQUOR STORE, GOLDEN EAGLE, WHICH ADDED TO A GREAT DEAL OF SURROUNDING TRAFFIC AND A LOT OF LATE NIGHT NOISE

ED MCNEELY CLOTHIER Just across the street from the Pawnee in a building that once housed a newspaper where Mrs. Chamberlin worked. There will be more information on this later in the book.

Ed was an outfitter years before and had a great old clothier building with boots, hats, cloths, as well as a great line of gift items. Ed was a great story teller while you sat around an old pop bellied stove in the winter to keep warm. When Ed started cleaning out the building getting ready to close his business, I was helping him and to our amazement, we found box after box suppose to have new boots, were filled with old boots, that had been switched by some of his customers.

The following will be detailed in another section of this book

After finding many articles and pictures in the Chamberlin, I decided to do a complete research on the property, the Hotel, and the Original Court House.

CHAPTER 6

ORIGINAL COURT HOUSE

T HE ORIGINAL COURT House was in the building on the back North East side of the lot. This building is now a Duplex rented out as Apartments.

picture by Jo Jean DeHony

I DEVOTED MANY DAYS, hours, months trying to locate all of the actual facts, so I would make certain I did not embellish the story and to make sure to have this be a book used as history and facts. This will be filled in later, as the Duplex was the original court house, when it was offered to the Town Fathers by Dr. Chamberlin to be used until they could build a court House.

Remember: FACTS—NOT FICTION

CHAPTER 7

CHANGES

picture by Jo Jean DeHony

I HAD MY FAMILY up, to see my new purchase and mentioned a little room on top of the building. "I called it my Crazy Aunt Room" (an old saying with no background) but with the curiosity of what could possibly be in that little room with a tiny window. This is what he found. A great box of past history. We found an original menu from the Irma Hotel, a BURLINGTON INN KEY, dance cards used for Mrs. Chamberlin, Old cuff links, small flags, and numerous other items that I placed in a show case for the guest to enjoy for many years. I also donated several items to the historical archives in Cody.

A very interesting thing for me was that each room had SKELTON KEYS. A long thin key with the individually crafted head on the end, a number of different designs, that made each key used for a different lock. These keys would open most any door. I immediately changed the locks, USING THE

MODERN WIESER LOCKS AND KEYS. This was for the safety of my guest, and a changing of times.

I was thrilled to find an OLD BOTTLE OF LAUNDRY BLUING IN BASEMENT, bluing was used to whiten the sheets, and the location this was found was the room where they did all of the laundry. The laundry was gathered and washed after it was dropped down a laundry chute from second and first floor into the basement.

I also found SEVERAL OF THE OLDER ORIGINAL COKE COLA BOTTLES. I have kept them, and really have no idea how old they are.

I was still remodeling and trying to cover all the rips and tears in the ceiling from the tearing out to redo lighting, wiring and light fixtures. The old light fixtures were small globes, with hand painted flowers, but were small and did not emit enough light. This was when I decided to use 4 foot fluorescent lights, that gave more light in the halls. This is when I felt the dropped ceiling with the grids and 2 x 4 ceiling tiles would look nice. I did not think I could sheet-rock and texture, and this would be easy. I could do it myself. This was not done by just me, but my mother and a few other people were there to help when I needed an extra hand.

Guest enjoying the patio in the back yard of the Pawnee Hotel with the Annex and Duplex in the background

picture by Jo Jean DeHony

Guiding light

Graceful light fixtures remain in the long halls of the Pawnee. Years of hotel patrons found their rooms by this lamp's light.

It was not hard to guess what part would be remodeled last, and take the longest. It was the living quarters in the back of the hotel, where we lived and did not have to be available to the guest.

My mother lived with me and to help with the hotel. She got right in the middle of all of the remodeling and mess, and she was always such a great person to jump in and help and never complain of the mess we had in the room, kitchen, pantry and a bedroom with a private bath. This was wonderful and everything was slowly falling into shape.

We ripped out a shower and a divider in the kitchen and took 5 coats of old paint off the cupboards in the kitchen. The wood was beautiful under this paint, so we used a clear finish to bring out the wood texture. With this remodeling it made a much larger kitchen area.

At the time I started on the kitchen it was also the only place I could put the large washing machine, so that was the starting of tearing out a doorway, and enlarging it to a large archway, tearing out the windows in the living room to get the machine in to be taken into the kitchen area. When I started drilling into the floor to take the drain and plumbing into the basement, the jackhammer plunged down through the floor, and almost sucked me into the basement, and I had the drill bit stuck in the concrete. I could not get it to back out. I had to run to the electrician that had loaned me the jackhammer to ask how to get it out of the floor. He came down and made it look very easy, he just reversed the drill and pulled the large hammer bit out of the cement in the floor. I found It was a large slab of cement with a huge open space beneath it.

The wall was to be rebuilt and a doorway was to open into the next room. To my surprise I found that at some time there were windows to the outside, and the wall was covered with tin to protect the wood from the heat from the stove that was used to cook those great chicken dinners and bake those delicious pies that I have been told about so often. We knocked a hole in the wall for a door. I framed it up, paneled, and moved on to the next remodeling idea. The old large stove was used for heat in the back area and for cooking the dinners for the guest that ate in the hotel. These dinners were served when Mrs. Chamberlin owned the hotel. (Prior to the large stove being in the kitchen it was reported that Mrs. Chamberlin had a very nice cook stove shipped in and cooked outdoors near the kitchen and the serving area for the guests. I also was told that Mrs. Chamberlin had excellent fried chicken dinners every Sunday, and the people loved them. As we get to the back annex I will give you more information on the Chicken dinners and the barn.

When we took out the floor in the kitchen and found that a lot of work would need to be done to complete the remodeling of the kitchen, we spent several weeks walking on 2 x 12 planks with some plywood over them. Beneath those planks was a huge hole in the ground that possibly held a large tank or septic area, but had been removed and left the large hole, which I never found what it was used for. We often thought about all of the mess, wondering just how we could tackle the project and make it an enjoyable remodeling task, but then found many times we would be a little down hearted mainly because we did not have a floor. It was unhandy, dirty, and it seemed to take so long to get the kitchen remodeled, and to get our cooking facilities, a sink, water, and cupboards installed in order to finally use this room for a kitchen.

WE STARTED WITH BLACK AND WHITE TVS, THEN LATER COLOR AND CABLE WITH MORE STATIONS THAN ANYONE COULD EVER USE. TVS IN THE KITCHEN THE BEDROOMS, THE LOBBY, THE BEAUTY SHOP, THE FISH STORE, EVERYWHERE I COULD PUT ONE.

BRINGING TVS FROM BILLINGS When I first opened the hotel, I had gone to Billings and purchased a pickup load of Televisions. When I started across

Chapman Bench, the wind was blowing so hard, I could hardly hold the pickup on the road. Then without any warning it caught the Televisions and blew several out of the back of the pick-up. When I pulled into the barrow pit and stopped to see what damage was done, I found five boxes had blown off and all of the televisions were destroyed. I picked up the boxes and broken TV's and started on to Cody, and this would mean I would open the hotel with five fewer televisions. They were the first televisions, all black and white. But was much better and nicer than what had been in the rooms at the time I purchased the hotel.

JOHN AND FRED LIVING IN THE ANNEX When starting on the remodeling of the Annex, which was a two story building directly in back of the hotel, there was 4 small rooms, two down stairs, and 2 upstairs. These rooms were occupied by 4 older gentlemen that did not want anything to change. One moved immediately, and moved to Old Trail Town, the down stairs became available when I decided I had to remodel the entire building. The other man upstairs stayed, and I moved him downstairs while I was redoing the upstairs rooms. They had lived there for many years, and their electricity consisted of one of the twisted old time electrical wires, hanging from the ceiling, with a pull chain socket, and screwed into that was a double plug-in, with everything they could find plugged into that one wire. I was astonished that they had not burned down the building. After the remodeling and trying to make Fred comfortable, I decided he needed a new mattress, box springs and bed stand, but it really upset him, as the old mattress belonged to him and he had it for years and did not want to let it go. I told him the new mattress and bed was his new gift, and after that I hauled the old bed to the dump with the help of a gentleman. Thank heaven for his help as the wind caught the mattress near Beck Lake and blew it off the pickup, where we had to reload. I could never have lifted it by myself.

While Fred was living in the Annex, he was always asking if he could help in the yard or around the hotel. One bright and sunny day I told him to help me with the tomato plants, they need to be weeded, and the tomatoes were growing so well, they were putting on the first tomatoes, just leaving the green stage and starting into the ripening stage with the yellow color, I could hardly wait. Within a few minutes Fred came into the hotel and told me he had pulled all of those tomatoes up as they were turning yellow and apparently had a disease. I was so upset that I told him they were ripening and please do not help me in the yard anymore.

BED IN BACK OF GARAGE One part of the annex was a garage, and an elderly gentleman was sleeping in the back of it in a little area large enough for a bed, and some cloths.

HORSE BARN AND CHICKENS This Garage, had at one time been the horse barn, and I was told that the horses for the fire wagon was kept there, and later Mrs. Chamberlin kept her chickens in this area, so when she had the Sunday chicken dinners she would just go out back, and get a nice plump chicken, dress It, and get it ready to fry.

THE GARAGE BEHIND THE HOTEL that was later turned into my laundry room with two large washers and a dryer for the hotel linens. The man that lived there had passed away so his bed and belongings were disposed of as he had no family. His little area was later an addition to the apartment in the annex located to the back of the garage and backing up the present apartment and later became a very small kitchen and part of a bathroom.

picture by Jo Jean DeHony

Approximately 1 year after the original purchase of the hotel and two lots, I decided I needed the last remaining lot on the North end with the small duplex located on the East corner. I proceeded with the plan to obtain money, and check to see if the original owner would sell. They told me that they thought it would only be the right thing for me to have that lot, as it all went together, so plans were made. The lot was purchased, and after a couple of years I fenced the entire property, and started a lawn in the vacant ground on the North end of the Property. I did not think anything would grow there as it had been vacant for so long, and the ground was as hard as a nail. I plowed, hauled in dirt, planted and watered and watered day in and day out, and when the first sprig of grass came up, I was delighted. Then I continued to plant trees, flowers and a garden. This was the time I ran into some bricks and rocks on the West end of the Duplex. I could not figure that out. There was no dirt, only rocks and bricks. What had they been used for? But I soon found out there had been a vault on the West end of the Duplex, and had been used for the first Court house in Cody, 1909. I dug out the rocks, spaded up the ground until it was fine soil and ready to be planted. Just West of this area, a couple who had lived in the Duplex, had been able to have a very nice small garden, so this just added more space, and it grew great tomatoes, and cucumbers.

After about 2 years, the lawn was growing, the trees were getting some size, and it was a beautiful lot, at the corner of 12th and Rumsey. We could sit on the Patio and enjoy the large garden area in the center of down town Cody.

I was approached to donate a space on the North West corner of the lot for a bench so that the senior citizens from the manor as well as other persons walking from the west end of town (when walking to the grocery store), or a shopping area, would be able to sit and rest. I agreed if the committee would supply and install the bench. They never found the time to do this small project, so it just remained part of the yard.

Another great disappointment after I had a nice yard, and it was costing a great deal to water, I approached the City to add me to the Raw Water lines that had been placed on every street in Cody, only to find out that the Pawnee on 12th street, and the City Hall in the next block had not been supplied with the water lines and Raw water. Guess What? The City sent a young man down with the water truck to water my lawn. I was totally amazed, as the big hose would have washed out all of my hard work. I told him not to even attempt to do that. So I continued to pay the high water bill to make the 12th and Rumsey street location a nice location, and a very nice addition for the beautification of Cody. Soon I was able to reach an agreement with the City to bill me through a separate meter for the water to use on the yard. The main meter was used as the City water for the hotel.

CHAPTER 8

THE BEAUTY SHOP

I STILL WANTED A beauty shop, "that's how this all started". On the North side of the hotel facing 12th street, was the ideal place for a beauty shop. I started tearing out the interior immediately and it was not long until I goofed, and took out a bearing wall. This really excited me and that was a hurry up and fix project. Extra help was needed to put in the large beams and support so I could continue tearing out the walls and getting the corner on the northwest end of the hotel remodeled to become the long awaited Beauty Shop.

I needed help to get the old plaster and lath torn out and was in a hurry to get this beauty shop opened. I had gone to a local bank, and they did not feel it would work so I just did it on my own. I hired a couple of men that was near Steck's grocery store and looking for work. They worked their tails off, ripping, loading and hauling to the dump. I soon had walls in, the wet stations were installed, and working just as planned. Then a nice room for hair dryers, a larger and well decorated room for the display and retail. I thought it was beautiful and we named it the PRETTY LADY BEAUTY SALON.

The entrance to the salon was through the front door of the hotel, and through a door immediately to the left as you entered the lobby. This entrance would work for several years and when the right time came I would make more changes and the entrance would change.

A new sign was installed, a large round globe with PRETTY LADY in very large print and in, smaller letters Beauty Salon.

In order to install this sign, we needed to drill through the brick walls, there were double walls, the front of pumice stone, that created a nice facing and then beneath the pumice stone was the old red brick from the original Hotel.

I had a young man staying in the room that was going to be drilled into. He was sitting in his room, on the bed, with his ear phones on, and into a world of his own.

They drilled through the wall, went into the room and bolted the sign from the inside of his room. They were not particularly quiet. It was all completed, and he never knew anything had happened. I could not believe he was unaware of this going on, but when he checked out a couple of weeks later, we were turning and cleaning the mattress, only to find many empty tubes of glue between the mattress and box springs. I learned that he was high on the smell produced from the glue. That was about the time when this was a popular thing for a lot of people to do.

I was so happy that it worked out and was opened on time. I made sure I sent the banker's wives, as well as the bankers that did not think this would work, "a special free hairdo of their choice". I wanted to prove it could be done and it would be successful. It was done and it was successful.

The Pretty Lady grew and was a very successful salon. I soon opened a door directly onto the sidewalk on the West side for private entrance.

Much to my surprise, as we tore into the wall and found there had been a door way (Dr. Chamberlin's dentist office) had been closed off at some time, so we just reopened it and saved the cutting out brick, building in doors and a lot of work.

After the beauty shop had been completed and opened I wanted the hotel to be beautiful so I decided to completely cover it with a white fiberglass coating, we put every window in new with double panes and screens, this made a big difference on appearance, and a lot warmer, as they were the old wooden frame and old screen windows, I wanted to put black wrought iron on the front over the windows and around the doors. It changed this building completely. I made sure all surrounding buildings were also covered and painted white, to offset the yard and the surrounding area of the Pawnee Hotel and the Pretty Lady Beauty Salon. What a beautiful change with a new look.

This led to more remodeling. I WAS THRILLED. I love to remodel. Several years later, the little court yard had been enclosed with a chain link fence and the back basement lift up door was closed off. This will lead to another section on this very project a little later. I opened a back door to the beauty shop and enlarged it into another room where we had a cobblestone street effect with the glazed brick walls. The cutting area was a wishing well with large white rocks, and a four way mirror on the top of the stand, one wet station, and beautiful new black hydraulic chairs. This room was made mostly for the men, so they felt they were as special as the ladies and had their own room.

The beauty shop remained for some time as a beauty shop, until I leased the front area out to the head Operator and she managed the shop for 15 years. She did not want the back room as she felt 4 wet stations and 6 dryer stations were large enough so we proceeded to close off the back room and started another venture, a tropical fish shop.

JO JEAN THOMAS DEHONY

CHAPTER 9

THE TROPICAL FISH SHOP

I CLOSED THE BACK room from the main salon, and made it another business. My mother and I put in a tropical fish store, and sold a lot of fish, tanks and supplies, and enjoyed each and every customer. The fish were shipped via airplane from Denver each week, and we always had a group of people awaiting their arrival, the hotel lobby would be full many nights and days while the people would wait for the new fish orders to be unpacked and readied for the time to purchase and take the new fish to their new homes.

They were good fish, healthy, and a good variety. My mother enjoyed the fish shop and the customers. This led to us being so interested in the fish that we started hatching and raising many of our own. We had 52 tanks in the little one room fish shop, 4 large tanks in the lobby, all full of a very large and nice selection of fish. We were busy sitting up tanks for people and some of the businesses that wanted a nice set up, for their business customers. Places like the nursing home, doctor offices and other areas that wanted the natural soothing effect you get from watching fish lazily swimming around in a beautiful atmosphere.

We had a great set up in the basement with a large filtration system and lights that killed disease or problems that you find in fish which helped our shop to be top notch in the healthy fish sales. But again we did have our share of water problems in the fish store, but easily fixed. A bucket and a good mop works wonders.

CHAPTER 10

NAME CHANGE

AFTER HAVING THE Pawnee for some time, I wanted to change the name from Hotel to "Pawnee Lodge". This led to updating it and changed the sign to a very nice White pod sign with Black letters. The old neon sign was a collector, but did not put out much light. The street in front of the hotel was dark and I wanted a street light, but at that time could not get one from the City. I thought the White pods would produce a nice lighted sidewalk, and it did. This was a great improvement for some time, and soon the City did put in a street light, what a change. It made us feel like we were part of down town Cody. In doing this they had to tear out a large portion of the side walk which caused up-heaval to the sidewalk. Several years later the whole sidewalk had to be redone, and leveled as it was causing people to trip and could have been dangerous. The City worked with me on getting this fixed. We now had a new smooth and attractive walk for the public, which also helped the appearance of the hotel.

This name "Pawnee Lodge" remained for several years until I decided too many guest calling in thought this was a Lodge, out of town similar to a guest ranch. This prompted me to change it back to Pawnee Hotel. I could easily do that by only changing Pods (letters) and it became the Pawnee Hotel again with the exception that one of the letters was put in backward and upside down. I left it that way for some time to see how many people noticed and believe me a lot noticed and called. I fixed it and the name "Pawnee Hotel" remained until it was sold in 2005 at which time the new owners changed the name to Chamberlin Inn.

I was still remodeling the rooms and trying to make sure each room had a bath or shower. When I purchased the Hotel, there were only about 5 rooms with their own bath and a central bath for the balance of the guest.

This became a challenge to give each room a shower or bath, and was a long process, but I continued to upgrade the Pawnee, and had so many wonderful guests. Most of the occupancy was created by word of mouth, repeat business, and the meeting of so many nice people. The popularity of the hotel grew and I enjoyed the nights with no vacancy and new guest. This continued throughout the time I enjoyed the ownership of the hotel.

The first remodeling to make certain each room had a private bath. This was a creation that I thought and wondered many times if it would work but it was accomplished by taking two adjoining rooms that had closets back to back, ripping out the wall between them, closing one room closet entrance, this making another room for a shower, sink and toilet. It worked great, with the closet being closed off and installed the hanging cloths racks, then used the second room that already had a large tub with its own bathroom for another private bathroom. This made a much more modern effect.

This type of remodeling continued. I took two rooms #16 and #18 with a large bathroom between, building an additional wall in the hall for a private entrance, and opening two rooms as a suite with a bathroom for the two separate rooms. This gave more privacy, and was to be utilized for a family, two couples, or the arrangements the guest chose Room #25. I then opened up the large closet in the hall which had been used for a large hat and shoe closet by the previous lady that ran the hotel. I installed a large tub, a dressing area, a shower, sink and stool. This became a very large and nice public bath. This would be used often if any room had only a shower or tub, and the guest preferred the opposite, they could just use the large beautiful public bath. This public bath was used many times for people that just needed a place to clean up in their travels and did not stay overnight. They would pay for the bath, and use of a towel, washcloth, and soap and left happy.

After all of the remodeling, I had only one room that did not have a shower, only a sink, and I still had a center room that did not have an outside view. It was a room in the middle of the building, and after using it as a room for many years, with its own shower, stool and sink, I decided to make it a room for the storage, towels, and supplies, as I felt everyone deserved an outside view. Another reason this room was change was a decision I made after a guest decided he wanted to see the water run out of the shower, and out on the floor. It fascinated him to watch the water run and feel it on his feet clear into the area where he was sitting on the bed. It had only one place to go, and that was through the ceiling into my living room, which had the nice popcorn texturing. It is easy to guess the ceiling fell off in large hunks when it got wet. This meant it had to be fixed, so I hired a contractor that could do this type of work as it was not easy, it had to be matched up, and it was a high ceiling with a lot of area.

While we were replacing the textured ceiling it lead to a lot of laughter even with the problem of having a mess. I had the contractor, for the professional work along with myself and two relatives working in the living room, holding the plastic to keep the texture off the carpet the furniture. This would prevent a big mess to clean up later. All of a sudden something happened and the contractor dumped a whole board of texture on the head of the relative, which caused a lot of laughs by some and not any from the victim. The only words spoken were, "Help Me" the other helpers and on-lookers, could not stop laughing, but during this laughter another statement made by the wife of the poor husband, with the texture dripping from his head, was " you look just like a giant condor just flew over." This has been a long standing joke, and talked about often.

It seemed we were building and moving every minute of the day, and the front check in area, was adorned with a new hand-made desk, then a short time later the stairway that went to second floor was carpeted with a beautiful old fashioned design to compliment the lobby.

Check in desk in front lobby of the Pawnee Hotel.
picture by Jo Jean DeHony

JO JEAN THOMAS DEHONY

picture by Jo Jean DeHony

The front South West part of the Lobby had a beautiful full glassed in porch that was used for many different ideas over the 31 plus years that I owned the Hotel.

At one time a very nice young business lady wanted a make up shop, and had that for some time. She fixed it up very nice and made an attractive addition to the present hotel. Shortly after she closed her shop and young man that was involved in gold and gems, opened a small shop, in the front lobby.

Another remodeling in the front lobby or sun-porch was just simply a room filled with plants, a phone, desk, table and benches for people to sit and to enjoy, have their lunch, coffee, a nice reading room, nice room to write letters, and was private, as they could shut the beautiful glass panel doors, that had been placed in their rightful place after they were discovered from their resting place for many years in the basement in the dark and dirty coal room.

CHAPTER 11

FIRST ATTEMPT TO WRITE A BOOK

IN 1982 AFTER many years of owning the hotel and wanting to publish a book or information on the hotel, I started with some of my experiences and named it :

SPOTS ON THE CEILING.

I sat down and typed and typed, and when finished I read it to my mother and a couple of friends visiting, and ask how it sounded: my mother said it sounded good to her, but it would take a long time to write my book, because everything I had written that day happened "last night". We all laughed, and I decided I would put it off until a later date:

I want to share with you my SPOTS ON THE CEILING that I started in 1982.

I not only want to dedicate this book to my Mother, Erma J. Thomas and Hannah Becquart the lady who has been a maid at the Pawnee Hotel for the past 25 years, but I must dedicate this book to these two patient, lovable and fun ladies.

My mother Mrs. Thomas has spent the past 8 years in the hotel, through joy, tough work, happiness, unusual happenings. And hours of pleasure from the variety of guest, traveling persons, all that have stayed with us. Each day Hannah and Erma, go through the daily routine of what's next and do we dare go into THAT room?

On Wednesday, a beautiful sunny day in June, the hotel was very busy with weekly and monthly rental request.

A very sophisticated lady Doctor, rented a room for two weeks, and at the time she was being given the instructions, that the room was changed, cleaned and made up once a week on weekly and monthly rental, she inquired has it been changed yet this week? This was of course the highlight for the hour, as the room is normally rented by the night, and is cleaned every day, with linen changes, and all that needs to be done for the next guest. This was a very light question. I did so want to mention the people the night before were very clean so it would be changed only on Tuesdays, but that would have been a rather bad joke, she might not have thought it funny.

On June 19, the hotel was a nightmare, with the busy City of Cody filled to capacity, and the traveling people madly bustling for a nights lodging, we encountered some very interesting happenings . . . First off we had the railroad call for a late reservation, and as usual try to provide the lodging for some of favorite people. Next the very nice manager of the Sunset Motel in Cody, called and had filled to capacity and wondered if there was room for three nice boys, for one night . . . Yes, one room with two double beds and a roll away . . . this was just perfect, and when they arrived they were three concessionaires for the carnival in town for the 4th of July, and decided they need the room for 6 nights . . . this was just great, and they were very happy to get such a nice large room and of all things with a huge bathtub . . . they preferred a shower . . . but what's new??

The next guest was a very nice young man arrived for a single, and having not stayed there before wondered of the room had a bath. Erma said, "yes it has a bath", the quest replied "then does it have a stool", "why yes it has a stool, have you ever seen a room with a bath and without a stool", and at that time she asked me which room, 15 or 26, since we had recently had a mishap from 15 upstairs directly above the counter, where we checked guest in. I said if he is going to stay give him 26, at that time he was more than amazed, and I showed him the ceiling directly above the counter. A LARGE SPOT ON THE CEILING . . . next to TWO MORE SPOTS ON THE CEILING and he asked if it was best to stand under the hole in the ceiling for his shower or could he go up-stairs . . . Erma again said, "you really better go upstairs".

Next, three elderly ladies from Minnesota arrived and were very upset over the mountains, and the driving through Yellowstone Park. Hungry, tired, scared, warm and late in all of their travel plans, so with about one hour of going over maps, and trying to help find a way home with NO MOUNTAINS, we finally decided to take the road to Billings and across 94 all the way home. They went to bed happy, tired, but much more at ease. You would never guess, while we were looking at the map the ceiling spring a leak over the kitchen stove, and through the large light, of course this had never happened before, and in trying to figure where it was coming from ? I soon found it was pouring in from #26 up stairs. I frantically ran up-stairs, knocked on the door, several times, very hard and no one answered . . . I then entered the room to find the problem and behold the couple was in bed and the man jumped up and started toward the door . . . I backed out and was yelling through the door. "We have a leak in the down stairs, please see if it is the shower or stool?" In about 1 second he reported he found it, and said it was the sink . . . they had plugged the sink and the faucet was running . . . therefore running all over the floor threw the floor, and ceiling into the kitchen downstairs. The maid, the next morning walked in water very deep in the nice plush rug, and then tried the rest of the day to dry it out for the next nights lodging guest . . . Another water problem, and another TWO SPOTS ON THE CEILING.

About 5 minutes later another young man arrived, and running short on single rooms, we gave him 15, the room with the shower that someone had broken the front panel and it therefore caused water to leak very badly into the Lobby, causing SPOTS ON THE CEILING. I explained to him he would have to use the public shower, bath and he was so gracious, and said no problem . . . He later came down and explained a very good way to fix this problem would be to rebuild the shower front with a nice fiber glass door.

Then the last two rooms of the evening was awaiting their special guests, and the phone rang a couple needed a room, but being the only two rooms left were# 16 an #18 with a share bath between . . . The rooms can be closed off and made into a suite. The nicely dressed gentleman arrived and was quite indignant that he should have to share a bath and said rather than do that he would just buy both rooms. HE DID JUST THAT! And of course he was not a happy person . . . I have been remodeling the bathroom between these two rooms and have not had the opportunity to hang the towel rack, and as he headed up the stairs, I asked him if he had time to go ahead and hang the towel rack and tissue holder. I believe he was surprised, but it broke the ice and he did decide he could talk and visit and he was from Honolulu Hawaii. The stool between #16 and #18 was recently replaced and are not the best to flush the water down, and only the night before I had replaced 8 large ceiling panels in the beauty shop, directly below these rooms, because they also had SPOTS ON THE CEILING.

I was swamped with people needing a room for the 4th of July and I did set up a lot of beds in rooms that were not finished only so they might have a place to stay.

I had mattresses and box springs stacked up in the lobby in two rows, almost to the ceiling, and believe me people were surprised when they came in and asked for a room. I told them to take a mattress and springs and I would show you a room. I really didn't have many takers but it wasn't long until as young man from Illinois wandered into the hotel, and needed a room for several days, he was put into #5, and stayed for a couple of weeks, and really did help move beds, a number of beds, and several other little jobs that came up. He came back almost every year, and almost every year, there were beds to move as I remodeled all of the time.

NOW WE WILL CONTINUE TO WRITE THE PRESENT BOOK.

PLEASE READ THE FOLLOWING CHAPTERS TO GET THE WHOLE STORY.

A VERY WELL STATED ADVERTISEMENT FOR
THE Pawnee Hotel
1032 12th St. • Cody, WY 82414
one: 307-587-2239 • 307-272-8829 • Fax: 307-587-2239

In the middle of down town Cody, Wyoming, 1/2 block off the main street of Sheridan Ave where The Irma and numerous downtown shops and resturants are located.

Picture by Ron Meyers for Jo Jean

The **Pawnee Hotel** is owned by Jo Jean DeHony. It is a perfect place to make reservations for a clean, quiet and comfortable stay, with a friendly atmosphere and reasonable rates. If you are looking for a special horse, booking with an outfitter, or just traveling through Wyoming, you will want to book your overnight stay in Cody, Wyoming at the Pawnee Hotel. Located in the Middle of Downtown Cody, 3 blocks from the Historical Buffalo Bill Museum.

The **Pawnee Hotel** was first established around 1900 under the name of Hotel Chamberlin, by Agnes Chamberlain.

As you enter the hotel, you will step into the second lobby area, where you will be greeted by our friendly staff.

After you register, you are able to look around in the lobby, to a step back in history, and find many interesting things to enjoy.

Our rates are very reasonable, and the hotel is Quiet, CLEAN and comfortable. Be sure and ask for a wake up call if you need to have one so you can start your day in exploring Cody. Or heading to Yellowstone Park.

The PAWNEE HOTEL is warm and comfortable in the winter. All rooms have either full or queen beds, showers, or large old fashion bath tubs.

We have designated non-smoking rooms, telephones in all rooms as well as a lobby phone and a pay phone.

No pets allowed, and arrangements must be made for coffee pots, or eating in rooms. Each room is decorated differently, and with a historical atmosphere. When you come to the **Pawnee Hotel**, bring your cameras because the Chief Joseph Highway is a journey of total beauty with the scenery. When you leave Cody going north toward Belfry you will see a sign 22 miles from Cody to turn left west on the Chief Joseph highway to continue toward Cooke City, Montana.

You will be surrounded by miles of beautiful scenery such as you have seen in photos. You can end up in

Yellowstone Park, Red Lodge Montana, or Cooke City Montana, for breakfast, lunch or dinner and return to your lodging in Cody for a restful evening.

While you are at the **Pawnee Hotel**, you have the convenience of many nearby restaurants and lounges.

All within walking distance. We do have a few restaurants that will deliver, but the weather in Cody always makes it a nice walk to any of the restaurants, or the Buffalo Bill Historical Museum, or a short drive to the Cody Night Rodeo during the season.

The following Pictures and descriptive text was taken from Wyoming Tales and Trails with their permission. For extensive history and information on Wyoming, be sure to look up "Wyoming Tales and Trails on you computer.

More pictures and information has been taken from the book Agnes Chamberlin written by Ester Johansson Murray, with her permission. Some pictures from the Park County Archives, and accounting from the Original Hotel Chamberlin Registers from 1917 given to the author by the previous owner Mary Edwards, along with many items found in the attic of the Hotel after being purchased by the Author.

I have inserted several pictures throughout this section to help you get a feel of what the area was like when Agnes and Mark moved from Hartville to Cody, as well as the Cody and Yellowstone Park area while they lived in Cody.

CHAPTER 12

DIFFERENT LOCATIONS OF AGNES AND MARK CHAMBERLIN

Written by Agnes Chamberlin

FINALLY MARK FOUND that Hartville, Wyoming might prove a profitable location, and he set up his practice there and wrote Agnes to join him, which she did in March of 1900. This was not Agnes' first encounter with Wyoming. In 1896, she had suffered two failed love affairs and contemplated suicide. Instead she accepted a job with I. O. Middaugh, in Wheatland, Wyoming, and worked five months on his paper.

Wheatland, another brand new town, whose post office dated from 1887, was linked to the east by the Colorado and Southern Railroad.

She liked Middaugh but could not get along with his wife so he had to let her go. She returned to Wichita, and took a course in a commercial collage before going to Woodward. Later, fate destined Middaugh to be murdered in a bank across the street from Agnes in Cody, Wyoming.

Unsettled

Ever since my arrival at Hartville, near old Fort Laramie, on March 17, I had been unsettled. It was evident that there was no future for Hartville (the following pictures and information on Hartville, has been added to show you what it was like around the time the Chamberlins' were living in that area and no pictures for Guernsey, which was just being settled at what was then the western terminus of the Burlington railroad, so when we were offered the team and wagon and dog very cheap, we accepted the offer and started out to look for a location. We thought we would go to Thermopolis, of which we had heard a good deal, and if it did not look favorable to us, we would go back and locate in Casper, which had plenty of dentist already, but might be forced to make room for us if nothing better offered. After we left Casper, going toward Thermopolis, we kept hearing about the new town of Cody which Buffalo Bill was promoting, and that the Burlington railroad was building into there.

The following pictures are of Wheatland, taken around the time Agnes Chamberlin, spent 5 months there in 1897, and worked for I. O. Middaugh, editor of the newspaper, *The Wheatland World*.

Gilchrist Avenue, looking west, 1908.
courtesy of Wyoming Tales and Trails

The building on the right in the above photo is the Globe Hotel at the intersection of Gilchrist Ave. and 9th Street. The two-story building on the left is the Carey Block. The building on the left at the bottom of the photo is the railway depot. The hotel was constructed in 1894 and was ultimately razed in order to construct a parking lot.

Wheatland Depot
courtesy of Wyoming Tales and Trails

The Railroad Depot, located at the east end of Gilchrist Avenue, was constructed in 1895 and is now on the National Register. The Depot closed in 1969.

Hartville, 1898
courtesy of Wyoming Tales and Trails

Mining in the Hartville Range, however, preceded the coming of the Sunrise Mine. Nor was Sunrise the only iron mine in the area. In the 1880's there was copper mining centered on Hartville. Nearby was Ironton, the mining camp for the Chicago Mine. In 1878, John Fields, the manager of the stage station at Government Farm, 14 miles north of Fort Laramie discovered an abandoned copper mine. Fields was later appointed by the government as the temporary custodian of Fort Laramie upon its abandonment. It was speculated that the mine had been that of earlier fur trappers or Indians. By 1881, there was a rush of miners into the area and by 1884 the town of Hartville arose, named after Major (Brevet Lt. Col). Verling K. Hart who also located copper deposits in the area. But by 1887, the copper rush had ended and the attention of miners turned to onyx and iron.

Hartville, 1899
Courtesy of Wyoming Tales and Trails

IN 1897, the Blue Bird and Good Fortune iron mines opened. The Good Fortune was owned by Joseph J. Hauphoff and Ichabod S. Bartlett. Bartlett later was the editor of the *History of Wyoming*, S. J. Clarke Publishing Company, Chicago, 1918. Hauphoff, before coming to the Fort Laramie/Hartville Range area of Wyoming, was a saloonist and shoe store proprietor in Cheyenne. Later he operated hotels at Fort Laramie and Badger. Badger, named for Assistant Postmaster General George Badger, was located where the Cheyenne and Northern crossed Cottonwood Creek. The town basically consisted of a general store and Haughoff's hotel, the "Badger House," a one-story affair. Before statehood, Hauphoff served as a United States Commissioner and later as a justice-of-the-peace. The later office gave him the honorary title of "judge." A. W. Bowen in his 1901 *Progressive Men of Wyoming* described Hauphoff as being "universal popular," perhaps a slight exaggeration. In August 1895, *The Salt Lake Herald* reported that "Judge" Hauphoff survived an attempted assassination. After the establishment of the mines at Hartville, Hauphoff maintained ownership of the scales, a source of unhappiness with the ore haulers who were paid by the ton. In Feburary, 1998, Hauphoff was beseiged at his scales by unhappy ore haulers who attempted to take over control of the scales. Hauphoff held the ore haulers off with a Winchester. Nevertheless, it was necessary for the sheriff to travel from Cheyenne to calm the situation.

One difficulty for mining in Hartville was the absence of a railroad. In 1896, Luke Voorhees (1835-1925), former manager of the Deadwood stage line, received the contract to haul the ore from Hartville to Badger using 10 ore wagons and sixty horses. In the meantime, three different companies began a race to provide rail service to Hartville. In 1897, there was discussion of the Union Pacific, Denver & Gulf constructing a spur. The only difficulty was that the line was in receivership and it would require court approval.

Hartville, 1926
Courtesy of Wyoming Tales and Trails

In 1899, the Burlington began construction of an extension from Alliance, Nebraska to Hartville. Delays, however, were encountered. On May 13, 1899, officials of the Colorado Fuel and Iron Company, by then the operators of the mines at Sunrise, incorporated the Colorado and Wyoming Railroad. The announced intention was to construct a line from the Cheyenne and Northern to Hartville. In the meantime, the Denver and Gulf closed its mines in Hartville. In 1900, the railroads arrived at Hartville. With the arrival of the railroads, Badger faded into non-existence, its site marked by reddish soil from the spillage from the ore wagons and remembered only in the name of a road and a voting precinct.

Sunday School class in front of Hartville School, 1900
Courtesy of Wyoming Tales and Trails

AGNES CHAMBERLIN AND ON TO THE HOTEL CHAMBERLIN

CHAPTER 13

EARLY LIFE IN CODY

AGNES CHAMBERLIN WITH A FISH SHE CAUGHT

Cody, Wyoming, 1897.
Courtesy of Wyoming Tales and Trails

TO THE WEST of present-day Cody, just south of Rattlesnake Mountain, the South and North Forks of the Sinking Water River (now, by act of the Legislature, known as the Shoshone) combine. The stream then flows northeastward past some suphurous hot springs now named after an early settler Charles DeMaris who arrived in the area about 1888 and proved up his homestead in 1894. Early mountain men named the river from the characteristic aroma emitted by the springs. Indeed, early hunters noted that the smell of the springs was perceptible several miles downstream. The river ultimately unites with the Bighorn east of Lovell. The Bighorn in turn flows into the Yellowstone continuing northwest across Montana until it combines with the Missouri in North Dakota. To the northwest of Cody arises Skull Creek a tributary of Pat O'Hara Creek which in turn feeds into the Clark's Fork.

The Shoshone River, originally named "Stinking Water" by the Crow, clearly showed irrigation potential. In 1895, Cody, George T. Beck, Cody's Wild West show partner Nate Salsbury, Harry Gerrans, Bronson Rumsey, Horace Alger, and George Bleistein founded the Shoshone Land and Irrigation Company. That year a town site was laid out near DeMaris Hot Springs, two miles west of present-day Cody.

However, Beck did not like the location or the fact that a great deal of the land was already owned by Charles DeMaris. And DeMaris was not interested in selling. Beck began looking at other possibilities to the east and soon settled on the town's present location. In the fall of 1895, construction began on the Cody Canal, which would carry water from the south fork of the Shoshone River northeast to the town. In May 1896, Beck and surveyor Charles Hayden laid out the site of the present town

Some said the place held great promise, and others said it was only a Mormon settlement that did not amount to anything, and the railroad was not going there at all, but was heading up the Big Horn River to Basin and Thermopolis. We stayed a month at Thermopolis and then on the strength of all the reports we could get on the place, and especially on account of the appearance of the Cody Enterprise, we decided to come over here and have a look for ourselves. The evening we arrived, after putting up the team and getting some of our things into our room, Dr. Chamberlin made a tour of the town to see what the prospects were for work in his line. In an hour he came back

JO JEAN THOMAS DEHONY

delighted with the reception he had received from everyone with whom he spoke. Jake Schwoob was most cordial and made the first suggestion that we locate here.

Cody, Wyoming, approximately 1900.
Courtesy of Wyoming Tales and Trails

Although the Town of Cody had less than 50 buildings at the time of the opening of the Irma Hotel, and ten of those buildings were saloons, the town was equipped with the latest modern amenities including electricity, and a water and sewer system. Note the water tank on top of the hill in the above photo. The town remained, however, primarily agricultural, spurred on in part by the Col. Cody's Shoshone Land and Irrigation Company.

Written by Agnes Chamberlin

Late in the afternoon of August 26th, in the year 1900, there drove up in front of the old Cody Hotel a discouraged looking old team, one a bay and the other a grey, hitched to a small covered wagon and followed by a speckled pointer dog. A good-looking man of thirty-five alighted and went in to inquire for accommodations for the night for himself and his wife. Fortunately the front bedroom downstairs, one of the two guest rooms the house had finished for guests at that time, was vacant. The regular occupant of this room was the forest supervisor, who with his new wife were on a horseback trip over the Shoshone forest and would not be back for two weeks. Therefore the travelers might have the room until the honeymooners got back. This haven of rest was gratefully accepted by the travel-weary strangers, and in this modest and unpretentious manner did Dr Mark Chamberlin and I enter upon what turned out to be our permanent residence in Cody.

He met Mr. Peake, who edited the Enterprise and made the first suggestion that we locate here. From others he was informed that there had been no traveling dentist here for two years, and there was lots of work to be done.

Written by Agnes Chamberlin

Mr. C. E. Hayden had had a brother here who was a barber and he had built an office for him on the lot where the Methodist church now stands. He had gone away, but his office chair and some other things were there and Mr. Hayden rented us the office for as long as we wanted it. In a few days Hud Darrah came to town with a load of lumber from the saw mill he and Ora Sonners were operating on Carter Mountain. He needed a lot of dental work done and offered to exchange lumber for the work. Mr. Beck had a lot on Main Street that he would sell for one hundred dollars, so we decided to take a chance on the railroad coming and settle down here, for the present at least. We took Mr. Beck's lot and Mr. Darrah's lumber, and by straining our credit almost to the breaking point put up the first unit of the building where the Park Café now is. Gus Holms and his father were the only carpenters here then and they built the house while Dr. Chamberlin worked on people's teeth for the money to complete it and I took the dog and .22 rifle and went out into the hills and learned to shoot rabbits.

BEFORE RAILROAD

This was over a year before the railroad was built in here, so there were not many people here at that time. The northern limit of the settlement was a little tar-paper house standing about three blocks north of where the Pioneer building now is. The western limit was Mr. Beck's house, which consisted of what is now the Beck dining room and kitchen. There was nothing between the Cody Trading Company's building and Mr. Beck's house except Mr. Hayden's little house which stood about where his present residence is. Some people by the name of Ketcham lived in the old Bowermaster rooming house and their little girl was the only child in town except Betty Beck, who was not quite two years old when I first made her acquaintance. Mr. And Mrs. John L. Burns lived in a little slab house where the Arthur Evans residence now is. Mr. And Mrs. Walter

Schwoob lived in the same house they live in now, except they built on the east wing after I came here. Mr. And Mrs. Jake Schwoob lived where the Schwoob residence is now, and the front room is part of the old original house, part of it having been moved away later. Mr. And Mrs. Peake and Mr. And Mrs. Blaine and the Cody Enterprise were all housed in log shanties on the front of the lots where the old Buffalo Bill Barn was. This is about where the Diamond Lumber Company has its office and yards. M. O. Newton lived where Mrs. Newton now lives, and he built on the large log addition at the back of the house after I came here. Mr. And Mrs. Houx lived in the little log house that still stands empty just south of Mrs. Minnnie Williams's house in the south part of town. Mr. And Mrs. Webster lived and kept the post office in the house on the corner west of the Methodist Church. Mr. Beck's office stood on the corner where the Pioneer building now is and the building he occupied than is part of the present Green Front club room. There were two saloons, one run by Ben and Fred Primm on the lot and in the same building used now by the Buffalo Bill Oil Co. The other was in a building near where Campbell brothers' blacksmith shop now is Mr. and Mrs Ben Primm Lived in a little house about where the vacant lot is east of the Cody Hotel. That Winter Gus Holms built the building now occupied by the barber shop there. That is practically all the people and buildings there were at that time.

Jake Schwoob with hand on headlamp, license plate No. 1, approx. 1913
Courtesy of Wyoming Tales and Trails

Written by Agnes Chamberlin

As I have before indicated, the hopefulness and progressive spirit of the men and the urbanity and cordiality of everybody was so different from anything we had met within Wyoming, we felt we wanted to stay here among these fine people and take a chance on making a success of it. It was not long before we moved into our little house—dental office in the front room and living quarters in the back room–but after the first burst of dental work there was very little for Dr. Chamberlin to do that winter. The inactivity irked us so that I went to see Mr. Peake and got a job of setting type, which had been my occupation for several years before I was married. That winter and for the next three years I worked in printing offices most of the time until the spring of 1904 we built a two-story house on the lot where the Hotel Chamberlin now stands and I began keeping boarders. That winter the wind blew harder and more constantly than I have ever seen it blow since. One evening when it was time for me to quit work at the printing office, I waited until there was a lull in the wind before I started to fact it home. When I finally did start out, I made a run for the nearest building and waited behind it until there came another lull, when I made a final dash for home, Another evening Dr. Chamberlin and another gentleman came for me and escorted me home betweem them for fear I would be blown away. Forday after day the wind would blow pebbles onto the roof and we would hear them rattle down over the shingles and fall off onto the ground.

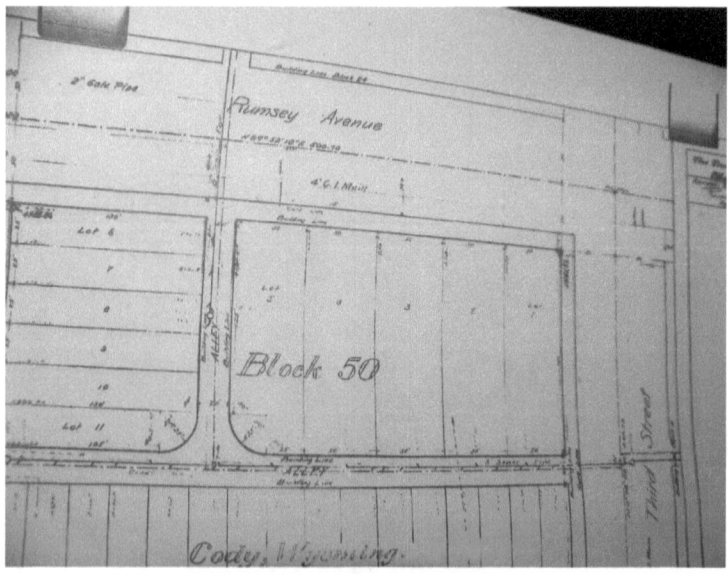

Park County Archives

Much of the Town of Cody was constructed by a friend of Cody from Buffalo, N. Y, Henry Montgomery Gerrans (1853-1939). Gerrans was a director of the 1901 Pan American Exposition in Buffalo at which the Wild West Show performed. The Buffalo, N. Y., influence on the Town of Cody is perhaps also reflected in the name of three streets, Gerrans Ave., Bleistein Ave. and Rumsey Ave. George Bleistein was also a director of the Exposition. The Rumsey family farm was used as a site for the Exposition. Beck, Alger, George Bleistein, H. M. Gerrans, Bronson Rumsey, II, are all regarded as the co-founders of the Town. Also moving to Cody from Buffalo, New York was Jacob M. "Jake" Schwoob (1874-1932) who became a partner and manager of the Cody Trading Company on the corner of 13th and Sheridan Ave.

Cody Trading Company, approx. 1911. Photo by A. G. Lucier
Courtesy of Wyoming Tales and Trails

The building depicted burned in 1913 and was replaced by a new building on the same site. Schwoob became the first treasurer of the Town of Cody. Two years later he was elected mayor. In 1905 he was elected to the State Senate and became president of the Senate in 1911. When Wyoming introduced license plates in 1913, he was given license plate No. 1.

PRIMITIVE

Housekeeping in those days was a very primitive business. The Cody Trading Company was the only store in the place, and it got its main bulk of supplies twice a year, in the spring and in the fall. At the time we arrived, supplies were pretty low and we had to take what we could in the way of housekeeping equipment. When our little house was finished, there was not a stove to be had at the store, nor any stove pipe either, so that we could not even set up our little camp stove in the house. When we moved in, we set the camp stove on the ground outside the kitchen window and when the meal was cooked we set the food onto the table inside the window and ate it in state. In the midst of this domestic tranquility there came a cold spell with snow. At once Dr. Chamberlin set out hunting for elk, but before he left he set the top box of the wagon, which had the cover still attached, on the ground at the east side of the house out of the wind and cut a hole in the top for the short stovepipe to project through and all through his absence I spent the day sitting in the covered wagon top by the stove knitting. After he came back, Dr. Gillam came over to see how we were getting along and was horrified to see that out house was so cold. He declared that he knew there was some stovepipe in the store, but everything was so mixed up there that they did not know what they had. So he and Dr. Chamberlin went to the store and hunted until they found enough stove-pipe to connect up our camp stove with the metal pipe which went through the roof. (There were no brick chimneys those days and by putting the stove on a box to make it a proper height for cooking, we were warm and comfortable in our new home. This was luxury indeed, to live in a house and have a stove to cook on. Stoves were expected any day, for Lon Shipp had set out from Red Lodge two weeks before with eight horses and three wagons laden with supplies for the Trading Company. Where he put in so much time on the way has always been a mystery to me, for Red Lodge was no further away then than it is now, and I am informed the distance is only sixty-five miles. At last after about two weeks more, one night after dark we heard a commotion in the street and went out to see what it was all about. Behold, it was Lon Shipp at last, and the next day there was set up in our humble home a real iron stove with dampers and legs and everything. What biscuits is baked, and even pies made of dried apples and such other primitive materials as I could get together. This was home at last, after a summer of wandering.

Stage at entrance to Irma Hotel, 1906.
Note shadow of upper porch railing on the sidewalk. porch
Courtesy of Wyoming Tales and Trails

The Cody Meeteetse Thermopolis Stage Line offered stage service south out of Cody. Additionally, there was weekly stage service to Painter in the Sunlight Basin to the northeast of Cody. By 1908 it was proposed to use auto-stages for the trip to Meeteetse. In 1908, also, the Big Horn Development company purchased six seven-passenger Rambler automobiles to provide transportation to Basin. In 1916, auto-stages were instituted to Yellowstone.

NO VARIETY

That first year and a half the variety of foods was very limited. There was no meat market, and the only way we ever got any fresh meat was when some rancher would kill a beef, and bring it to town and sell it to Mr. Marx, who ran the Cody Hotel. Then those of us who had influence with Mr. Marx would persuade him to sell us a little piece. The only other meat was bacon, and occasionally ham, pieced out with rabbits and elk meat. Of course Dr. Chamberlin shot his elk and we thought we had our winter's supply of meat, but alas, the blow flies spoiled most of it, as we did not know then about canning meat. There were no cans anyway, so it was just as well we did not know about it. There was no fresh fruit of any kind ever, except when the freight wagons came in and brought some oranges and bananas. There were no vegetables except potatoes and onions, and no one thought of having eggs, or milk, as there were no such things. No one kept chickens, and the store did not get in packed eggs, as they would have spoiled before they got here from the railroad. Mr. Peake kept a cow, and after I had lived here a good many months, one person who had been getting milk regularly moved away and I had the privilege of falling heir to their quart a day. The most enterprising of us used to go out in the fall and gather buffalo berries and make jelly, but we never got many berries because they were so hard to get and tedious to clean afterwards. After the railroad came in, in the fall of 1901 Mr. And Mrs. Yates came here from Colorado and opened a fruit store and after that fresh fruit and vegetables could be had all the year in ever increasing variety and quantity. Also about that time Mr. Larson came here and opened a meat market in the building just east of the Park Café and we were never again without fresh meat.

NO CLOTHES

When Dr. Chamberlin and I left Hartville, we had to leave behind my trunk and a few pieces of furniture, so I had no clothes with me except what I brought in the wagon in an old telescope. This was a campaign year and Mr. Mondell was running for re-election to Congress. All public meetings we attended were held in the north wing of the Trading Company's store, which was not much of a place but was available until the fall stores of freight came in. Several meetings were held there this fall, each one followed by a dance, but all I got out of it was lying awake at night and listening to the music and hearing people going back and forth through our back yard, for I had no party clothes. At last, after the campaign was over, my trunk came and I had one or two dresses from my wedding outfit left and was very presentable for social affairs for the rest of the winter.

My first party came late in the winter or the next spring. I cannot remember which. Mr. Beck thought we ought to have a men's club here and proceeded to round up all the men and organize the Cody club, the forerunner of the present Cody Club, although this was not a business Men's organization, but a "sportsmen's club." The first meeting was held in Mr. Beck's office, which stood where the Pioneer Building now stands. From my little house across the street the laughter and shouting sounded as though they had all gone crazy. Since then I have always remembered when people have told me about an occasion when "Everybody was drunk," how those men sounded on that first night to the ears of an outsider. The next month they had "Ladies Night," and I was there with the rest, and there was just as much laughter and uproar as the proceeding night, but I knew from observation that nobody was drunk. Those were great days for the married woman, for at this first "Ladies' night" there were only two unmarried ladies present for they were the only ones in town. They were Hattie McFall and a young lady by the name of Campbell, whose people had just moved here from Montana. They stayed but a few years and then went back to Montana, while I understand Hattie McFall is married and living on the west coast somewhere. This was the most important gathering until the opening of the Irma Hotel in the fall of 1902.

Information taken from research on individuals

Conant S. Parks

He is one of the leading men in the control of the First National Bank of Thermopolis, and is also one of the directors conducting the banking house of Amoretti Parks & Co., of Cody.

On each side of his house descended from a long line of distinguished ancestors, S. Conant Parks the genial and companionable vice-president of the First National Bank of Lander, Wyoming, exemplifies in his daily life the characteristics of good citizenship which have given so many of his family prominence and public regard. He was born at Auburn, Illinois on May 15, 1859, the son of Thomas S. and Nancy C. (Polley) Parks, the father a native of Indiana born on May 22, 1822, and the mother of Muhlenberg County, Kentucky born on March 24, 1828. The father of Mr. Parks was the president of the leading bank at Auburn, Illinois and a prominent man in the public affairs of that section of the country. He died at the ripe age of sixty-nine years, on January 28, 1891, at Auburn, where most of his life of mercantile and public usefulness had passed, and where his widow still resides. In 1888 after finishing his course of instruction at the noted German school, he came to Wyoming and locating at Lander, became the vice-president of a private bank in that city, which in 1892 was reorganized as the first National Bank of Lander. Of this institution he is still a director and the vice-president having in addition to the duties connected therewith a number of business connections of importance. To every enterprise in which he takes an interest he gives devoted attention making it feel the quickening impulse of his master hand. In fraternal relations he has ascended the Masonic ladder through the lodge chapter and commandary.

RAILROAD

With the coming of the railroad, people began to come in and start up several different lines of businesses. The year before the railroad came, Mr. Conant Parks, F. M. Williams and Mr. Amoretti came over from Lander and opened the first bank in Cody in the east Wing of the Cody Trading Company's building. After the railroad came, Mr. Fred Barmett came from Illinois with his family and shared with Frank Williams and Mr. S. C. Parks, Jr., the operation of the bank. The McGuffey Brothers came from Nebraska and opened the first Hardware store here. George Pulley came from Iowa and opened another general store, and at long last Mr. Arnold moved his store from a point just opposite the springs into town. Before that, he and his wife used to come into town with their team and deliver groceries to people who cared to order from them. All these businesses, together with several saloons, erected buildings on the south side of the block just west of the Cody Trading Company. Soon afterwards the stone buildings on the north side of the block which are still there were put up and the place began to look like a town. This story includes about that might be of public interest in my personal part in settling in Cody. The old files of the Enterprise will record what is of more public interest better than I can.

National Currency Blog—Eugene Amoretti, Wyoming's Banker

The West is famous as the home of outlaws and sheriffs. However, for every famous gun slinging law man there are another dozen men who were equally important to a town's success. In order for a new town to thrive it needed a few things: a post office, general store, doctor, and in most cases, a bank. Running a bank was complicated. It required capital and sound management. Often times only a few individuals in an area were qualified to do the work. During the national bank note issuing period (1863-1935) no one man in Wyoming held more national banking titles than Eugene Amoretti:

1892—First President of The First National Bank of Lander, Wyoming

1901—First President of The First National Bank of Thermopolis, Wyoming

1905—First President of The Shoshoni National Bank of Cody, Wyoming

JO JEAN THOMAS DEHONY

Eugene Amoretti's obituary is included below. It has plenty of details about his personal life and achievements. I want to focus on his family and the national bank notes he signed. Most people in the hobby realize that the greatest and most unlikely survivors from the national bank note period were saved by the bankers who signed them. These notes make their way to collectors in any number of ways, but almost always the grandchildren and great-grandchildren of the signers are responsible for relinquishing them. Sadly, the middlemen between the banking family and the collector can be coin shops, museums, and auction houses. The details of who originally saved important bank notes are traditionally lost over the course of time. The following is a discussion of what might have happened to Eugene Amoretti's currency he signed.

First National Bank, Lander.

E. AMORETTI, *President.*   ·   No. 4720.   S. C. PARKS. JR., *Cashier.*

FIRST NATIONAL BANK

LANDER.WYO..

M E M O R A N D U M

TRANSLATION

GLENROCK 10/22-1901.

My good Madam Clara H. Parks:

I send you one bill of the Bank of Thermopolis National Bank to my little Harold
prince, son. Keep it as a souvenir. E. A.

My good little friend, I am sending you
the first bill signed of the Thermopolis
bank. Accept my good and pleasant remembrance,
and may God protect you in your studies,
and you will become a great orator.

E. Amoretti

—A serial #3 note from The First National Bank of Thermopolis, Wyoming was given to the son of Samuel C Parks Jr by Eugene Amoretti in 1901.

Conversation: Samuel C Parks was the first cashier of The First National Bank of Lander, but he had no connection to the bank in Thermopolis. Why would Eugene Amoretti send Park's son this bank note? Perhaps E

Amoretti was aware that SC Parks had saved the first note from Lander and was simply adding to his collection. In the letter below, Eugene Amoretti tells Clara Parks that the enclosed note (serial #3) was the first note printed by Thermopolis. We of course know that the serial number one and two notes were printed and sent to Thermopolis.

If SC Parks saved the first note issued by Lander and then donated it to the museum, why wasn't the serial #3 note from Thermopolis also donated?

—Eugene Amoretti had two daughters. Margaret Amoretti died in 1923, having never been married. His other daughter, Eloise Amoretti Peck died in 1969, married but without children. Eloise's husband George Peck died in 1988 in Wyoming with no siblings, nieces, or nephews.

Conversation: Eloise Amoretti died just before the timeline was established for the serial #1 brown back from Lander's donation to the museum. If she was the donor and Eugene Amoretti the saver, why didn't he save serial number one notes from his other two banks?

The case of Eugene Amoretti and his three banks makes several points clear.

1) Don't donate important numismatic items to a museum.
2) Try to record history when possible. While it may not seem important at the time, 100 years from now someone might find it very interesting.
3) All kinds of banks and bankers had odd connections to each other. Some treasured bank notes and to others bank notes were just a means of commerce.

Time may never solve this case, but I think there is more to be learned and some important questions to be answered:

- What happened to the serial #1 and #2 notes from Thermopolis?
- Who originally saved the serial #1 note from Lander?
- Why has nothing important from The Shoshoni National Bank been discovered?

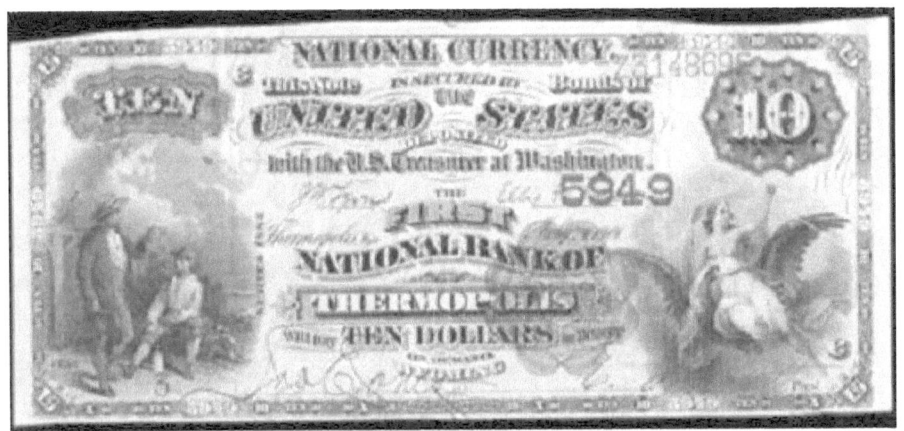

Wyoming State Journal, Lander, WY Thursday,
February 2, 1950 page 1 col 6-7

GENE AMORETTI DIES; HORSE CREEK RANCHER WAS ONE OF LANDER FOUNDERS

Eugene Amoretti, 79 year old pioneer of Fremont County, died Tuesday afternoon at 3 at his home, the EA Ranch, on Horse Creek near Dubois.

Mr. Amoretti, who had the distinction of being the first white child born at the gold mining area of South Pass, had been in failing health for several years. He was stricken ill one week ago, but on Monday was thought to be improving. However, he suffered a sudden relapse on Tuesday and death came within several hours.

At his bedside were his wife, and his son-in-law and daughter, Mr. and Mrs. George Peck. The end came at the ranch which he homesteaded a half-century ago.

FIRST WHITE CHILD

Mr. Amoretti was born at South Pass, son of Eugene and Mary Amoretti, on January 12, 1871. His parents, natives of Venice, Italy, came to the United States in the early 1840's and to Wyoming in 1868, going almost immediately to South Pass then a boom town as a result of gold discoveries.

Later the Amorettis came to Lander and Mr. Amoretti, Sr., and his son Eugene were prominently identified with the development of this town. In fact, Mr. Amoretti, Sr., often has been referred to by historians as the "Father of Lander, Wyo."

ATTENDED NOTRE DAME

Eugene or "Gene" as he was known to thousands, attended local public and private schools, and then was sent by his parents to Notre Dame University at South Bend, Ind. After studying at the famous institution, he transferred to the College of the Sacred Heart at Denver, and later studied also at the Friends College in Omaha. It was while in Omaha that he met and married Miss Eloise Creedon, who was the daughter of P. J. and Margaret Creedon, who came west from Pennsylvania.

The formal education that he received never took away young Amoretti's love for the West and the cattle ranges of his native Fremont and his education finished, he came back to Lander with his bride.

HOMESTEADED ON HORSE CREEK

Then followed a period of intense activity. He took up the 210 acres on Horse Creek, above Dubois, and started in the cattle business. Through the years he raised Herefords at the ranch and in later years also took dude during the summer months. It is one of the most picturesque ranches in the region. More recently the operations at EA Ranch have been in charge of Mrs. Amoretti and his son-in-law and daughter, the Pecks.

WAS ALSO A BANKER

In those younger years, Mr. Amoretti also was a banker, his father having launched the first banking business in Fremont County at the corner of Main and Third Streets, where the Noble Hotel now stands. This first structure was adobe and logs. The boy grew up in the mercantile-banking business with his father, and he branched out on his own, helping to organize banks in Thermopolis, Cody and Bridger, Mont. He served was vice president of the bank in Bridger.

Mr. Amoretti also held substantial interest in the Lander Electric Light Co., being its manager, and was manager of a roller mill in Lander. With his father, he engaged in extensive real estate developments in the town and county. Father and son encouraged me to homestead, to open farms and ranches, they laid out a town site known as the Amoretti Addition. Two streets are named in their honor—one Amoretti, and the other Eugene, both on the north side of town. The bank which the elder Amoretti established later became the First National Bank of Lander.

BUILT FIRST LODGE

Gene also constructed the first lodge in the Jackson Hole country, now the Jackson Lade Lodge. This he operated until about thirty years ago. It is on Yellowstone Highway, north or Moran.

Mr. Amoretti also took an active interest in civic affairs at Lander and Fremont County. He served as a member of Lander town council, and as a Republican was elected to two terms as County Treasurer. His father was a member of Wyoming's First Legislature, and Gene of the 19th and 20th State Legislatures sessions in 1927 and 1929.

RECALLED STIRING INCIDENTS

Mr. Amoretti recalled many stirring incidents in the early life of the region and of his boyhood. Where the post office now stands was a log cabin, in which two women made their home. One day, Gene recalled, Indians came into town, invaded the cabin, killed and scalped the two white women. A monument to their memory stands in the cemetery at Fort Washakie. Gene, then only boy saw the bodies.

He told other stores, too, of buffalo, and of a great abundance of wild game in the region, of the soldiers quartered here and later at Fort Washakie, of the Indians. hostile and friendly. They were happy and venturesome days for a boy.

WAS FRATERNALIST

He is survived by Mrs. Amoretti, and a daughter, Eloise, wife of George Peck, all of the EA Ranch. Another daughter, Margaret died in 1923.

Agnes Chamberlin worked for John Peake on the Cody Enterpris. The Cody Enterprise was established Buffalo Bill and John Peake in 1899. The first issue appeared on August 31, 1899, and it was firmly established in 1902. In 1904, it was bought by Caroline Lockhart, a Prohibition crusader and novelist originally from Boston. She served as owner and editor from 1904 to 1962 In the summer of 1936, it featured articles about artists Edward Thomas Grigwire and Stan Kershaw. It is now owned by Sage Publishing of Cody, Wyoming. It is published twice weekly.

THE FOLLOWING IS TAKEN WORD FOR WORD FROM ORIGIAL WRITINGS AND NEWSPAPER ARTICLES BY AGNES CHAMBERLIN

THE FIRST SPECIAL EDITION
OF THE ENTERPRISE

By Agnes B. Chamberlin

As the reader may easily imagine, the circumstances surrounding the issuance of the first special edition of the Enterprise were very different from those attending the present special edition. The date was December 22, 1904, and just why Mr. Peake, the editor, wanted to get out a special edition at this time cannot be recalled. There had nothing happened here that merited such a commemoration, but for reasons best known to himself Mr. Peake thought such an edition was due and he put forth every effort to get it out.

The paper was then housed in the building now occupied by Dave Shelley and was about as warm as a pasteboard box. The type stands and presses were in the back room, which was heated by a coal stove, which at the time was tended by anybody and everybody who got cold enough to get off his or her stool and fire up. The fuel was a wagonload of slack, which somebody had brought in to pay his subscription with, so we had to burn it, even if it did not warm up the place adequately. The wind blew just as it always does in Cody in December, shifting dust into our type cases and over the composing stones and galleys, to say nothing of cooling off the already chilly office. The force consisted of George Nelson, a very competent printer who had been with the Enterprise from the beginning; Bob McMullen, an old-timer here who had worked for the Enterprise off and on ever since it was started; another man who I cannot remember, and the writer that was called in extra for the special edition. We all took our lunches with Grandma Hurd, Mrs. Becks grandmother, who lived in the apartment upstairs in the same building. We went upstairs by the outside stairway, which Mrs. Shelley afterwards had enclosed, and each time would almost blow away in the high wind. In a letter recently to a friend here, Bob McMullen recalls some of the hardships of this experience as follows: "Yes, I well remember our Special Edition with a note of bitterness and chagrin. George Nelson got on a big drunk at the most critical time and left us in the lurch, with everything to do and shorthanded. I was over worked, time was pressing, the day of the grand finale was hourly drawing near. The boss was hysterical. I did not have the proper time to devote to the press work that should have been given to that particular job, with the result that the entire edition was "offset" and unreadable. Mr. Peake, in his eagerness for a glorious denouement, ordered a glazed paper, which was neither suitable for that old press nor the quality of ink which we had in stock. Nelson was aware of that fact and did not care to assume the responsibility of the presswork under the circumstances, so he sought refuge in the bosom of King Alcohol. We had depended so much on him and he signally failed us."

By some kind of fate, the copy of this edition which was providentially preserved for the files was not "offset", and is entirely readable and a very credible paper. However, the town was so small and new and there was so little to write about that it makes one wonder why the urgency for a special edition at that time. The paper comprised only ten pages, and the entire front page is given over to cuts and effusive padding about Cody and the entire Big Horn Basin. Mr. Peake was good at that, so the paper gives the impression of much larger and more advanced state of development then we really had. The rest of the paper is composed of advs. and the conventional write-ups of prominent people and rosy dreams about the future, such as gold, silver and copper mining; mining and processing betonite, borax, sulphur, potassium, etc.

Among the enterprises that got cuts and flattering write-ups may be mentioned. The two hotels, the Irma, operated by Col. Cody's nephew, Lance Decker; and the Heart Mountain Inn, Owned and operated by Mr. And Mrs. D. H. McFall, who long ago sold out and moved to the west coast and it is understood have both passed on.

Our first waterworks system, including the old pumping plant of blessed memory, on the riverbank, came in for an extensive write-up. We had voted the large sum of $16,000 for this improvement and were justly proud of it.

The first school house in Cody was a stone 2-room house which stood in the street just in front of the present cemetery. The town out grew it soon and the special edition contains a cut of the new schoolhouse, which is the back part of the present old grade school and cost all of $5,000.

The two banks, Amoretti, Parks & Co., and the First National, (the new bank) were lauded in pure 19th century style as "Sound financial institutions," which, thank heaven, in these uncertain times, they still are.

Cody's first murder of a prominent citizen, the cashier of the First National Bank, was given two full columns and illustrated by cuts of Mr. and Mrs. Walls, proprietors of the building where the bank was located, and Mr. Middaugh, the unfortunate only victim. This tragedy had occurred only six weeks before and was fresh in everybody's minds and was well written up. To this day no one has been convicted of this cold-blooded murder, although in the year following two different parties were arrested, exonerated and turned loose.

IRA O. MIDDAUGH

Few are there among the younger generation of business and professional men of the state of Wyoming who hold a higher place in the public esteem, or have brighter prospects for the future, than Hon. Ira O. Middaugh, the editor and popular proprietor of the Wheatland World of Wheatland.

He purchased the Plainville Times, which he conducted successfully until 1894. when he disposed of his interests in Kansas, and moved to Wheatland, Wyo. Here, in October, 1894, he issued the first number of the Wheatland World, a progressive and popular newspaper, which he conducted with great success from the date of its first issue. Its circulation gradually grew from year to year until it was among the largest of the country papers of the state.

Politically, Mr. Middaugh was a stanch adherent of the Republican party, The Wheatland World being one of the principal Republican organs of Wyoming. In 1896 Mr. Middaugh was elected a member of the Legislature of Wyoming from Laramie county and served a term in that capacity. In May, 1897, he was appointed postmaster at Wheatland.

At this time Agnes spent five months in Wheatland, Wyoming, working for I. O. Middaugh, editor the the newspaper, *The Wheatland Worl*

["Progressive Men of the State of Wyoming" . . . By A.W. Bowen & Co, pub. 1901—Sub. by Marie Miller]

The Name I. O. Middaugh, will appear several times throughout the story of Agnes and her enterprises in Cody, as well as information on the murder of a banker at a local bank.

The Oregon Basin irrigation project was about to become an actuality and was given three columns of encouragement, accompanied by cuts that show the enormous expanse of sagebrush that was Oregon Basin before the oil boom. Also there is a good cut of the Shoshoni Canyon before the government built the road on the north side preparatory to building the dam.

Under the heading, "Col. Cody's many interests," and subheadings, " The Magnificent Irma Hotel," "A Mammoth Barn" (The old Buffalo Bill Barn that was about where the diamond lumber Company now is;) "Several large ranches," The TE and Carter and Sweeney Ranches) Three columns of laudatory matter and three wood-cuts, one of Col. Cody himself, one of the Buffalo Bill Barn with the first 4-horse station wagon full of people and driven by Roy Meyers; and a priceless one of the Irma Hotel with the Canyon in its back yard, and an old stage-coach followed by a troop of horsemen coming around the corner. Unfortunately, these early woodcuts cannot now be found.

The newly formed Eagles' lodge had just elected new officers for the year, and they were R. A. Roth, Secy, and H.S. Ridgely, W.P., neither of whom does anybody but the oldest old-timers remember.

Among prominent citizens eulogized and honored with pictures are John E. Kearns, president of the Cody Lumber Co., Builder of the home occupied at present by W.T. Hogg, and in 1904 mayor of Cody: Hon. W.B Sleeper, who was state representative elect at this time, and only a few years ago passed on at his old home in Billings. He was the father of Marie Sleeper, of the movies, and lived in California many years before he died; F. C. Barnett, who came here to be president of the Cody Transportation Co., was later cashier of the Shoshoni National Bank, and who built the building where now is the Mayflower Cafe. He passed on this summer at Peoria, Ill., where he had been in the insurance business for many years. Also there is a picture of Carl Hammit, who was city marshal as long ago as that. Dr. Chamberlin was shown standing in front of his new office building and residence, which was just completed on the site where the present Chamberlin Hotel stands today.

There were lots of advertisers in the special edition, most of whom are gone today and have been for several years. Although this was only thirty-four years ago and the town don't seem to residents to change very fast, the only businesses that are here now that were here then, are the Irma Hotel, The Cody Trading Company and the Heart Mountain Inn; The Cody Enterprise, W.M. Loewer, our faithful mayor. Cody Lumber Co., now under the name of Diamond Lumber Co.; F.J. Hiscock, photographer, Cody Drug Co., and the two banks, which are practically under the same management as then.

JO JEAN THOMAS DEHONY

Frank L. Houx

Frank Lee Houx (December 12, 1854-April 3, 1941) was an American Politian, who served as the tenth Governor of Wyoming.

Houx married Augusta Camp in 1875, and sired two daughters and a son. (The birth year of Frank Houx is variously listed as 1854, 1859, and 1860; given his 1875 marriage, 1854 is Accepted.

He took up the study of law, reading in the office of John S. Blackwell, of Lexington, Missouri. Houx did not complete his course, however, turning his attention to commercial interests. He graduated from Shaw's Business College in Kansas City, Missouri in 1884. The next year, he moved to Montana and went into the cattle business. In 1895, he took up residence in Cody, Wyoming, where he went into politics.

On April 10, 1898, he was widowed. The next year, he remarried Ida Mason Christy, with whom he had four daughters.

For a time. Houx was associated with Col. William F. Cody (Buffalo Bill) in the construction of the Cody canal and other projects.

In 1901 when the town of Cody was incorporated, he first sought office, becoming the town's first Mayor. During his first term as Mayor, he also served as police judge from 1902 to 1903. He was re-elected to a second mayoral term in 1905. During the next four years, the town built a residence for him: this two-story A-frame building still stands and now serves as a bed and breakfast known as the "Mayor's Inn".

He sought election as governor in his own right in 1918, but was defeated by Robert D. Carey. Houx then went into the oil refining business in Texas but returned to Cody in 1935. He died in the famous Irma Hotel in Cody in 1941 at the age of 86, and was put to rest in Cody Cemetery. The autobiography he wrote in 1939 was published in serial form by the Cody Enterprise in the months following his death.

References

- Wyoming State Archives biography.
- National Governors Association biography

History Buff.com State Facts—Wyoming

Among the advertisers that have mostly passed on, or gone out of business, or left the country are: Frank L.Houx, Real-estate and insurance: F.M. Williams, real-estate and insurance; H. W. Darrah, coal and lumber; Mc Guffey Bros., hardware; Red Star Barn, D. H. Hutsonpillar ; A.S. Shirley, baggage and express; Nowlan's Restaurant, where the big juicy steaks grew; L. A. Townsend, photographer, successor to L.E Webster; G. McLaughlin, blacksmith; John L. Burns and R. A. Roth, saloons.

Out of eighteen advertisers in the Professional Cards column, the only persons living today are C. A. Zaring, of Basin, lawyer; C. Dana Carter, of Basin, now of Thermopolis, J. T. Bradbury, now of Willow Creek Montana: and J. H. Van Horne of Portland Oregon. Those who have passed on are:

Physicians Dr. L. Howe and Dr. Frances M. Lane.

Lawyers W. L. Walls, Ridgely & Van Horne; A. R. Williams, Blake and Lonabaugh of Sheridan, J. P. Arnott, of Basin, W. S. Metz of Sheridan; L. B. Reno of Chance, Mont.; Collins of Basin, Who was Zarings partner those days; C. E. Hayden and Joseph H. Neville, of Byron, both surveyors and U.S. Commissioners.

There is an admiring account of Miss Ruby Howe (now Mrs. George Pfrangle) going out with a party of friends and shooting a deer. Lady hunters were not as common those days as they have since become, and this prowess exhibited by a fourteen-year-old girl attracted much admiring comment.

—:—

Oct. 29, 1903, Fourteen carloads of sheep were shipped out of Cody for the St. Paul market by W. H. Pearce, Col. Picket and Allison & Bent. The latter were successors to J. W. Chapmen and predecessors of the Taggarts on the big ranch on Pat O'Hara creek. J. K. Barbee shipped two carloads of horses, and Wilson Bros, and George Merrill of Meeteetse, Shipped thirty carloads of cattle on the same date.

—:—

As long ago as 1903 surveys were being made for a reservoir site on the upper Greybull River. Thirty-five years from the inception of an idea to its fulfillment is a long time, but shows that somebody has faith as well as persistence.

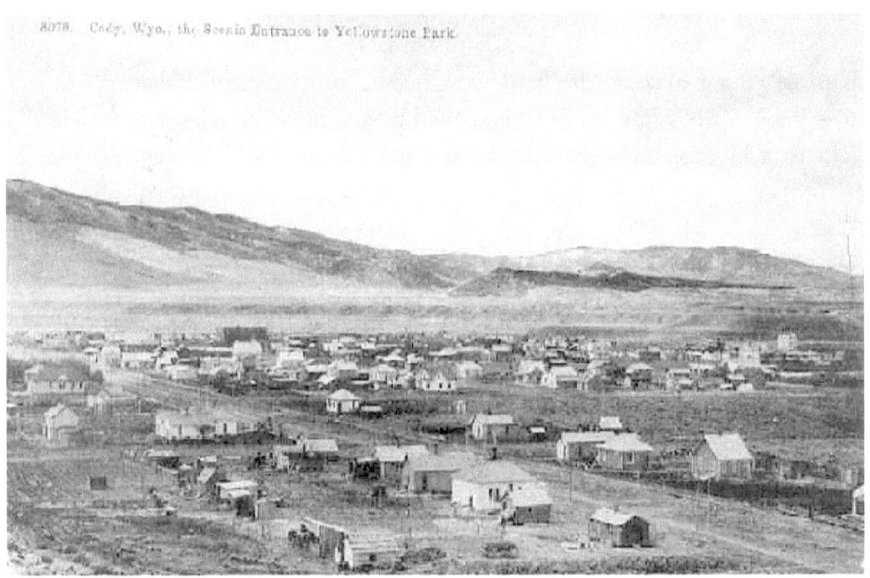

Courtesy of Wyoming Tales and Trails

CHAPTER 14

AGNES WRITES HER STORY

Business Ventures

Now we come to other business ventures of Chamberlain.

The above 1906 journal stated, "A flour mill was sorely needed in Cody". Mr. E. T. Cheese arrived in town with big ideas and promoted the flour mill by starting to raise the $25,000 needed to build the big square three story mill four blocks from the Irma hotel that would produce 125 barrels of flour a day. Even before the mill began production it advertised, "manufacturer of the Shoshone Chief Flour," and "Best roller mill in Wyoming" This is an example of the boosterism of the times. Even before it was started it carried the name "Home Industry Flour". This is an example of the boosterism of the times. The Shoshone Miling Company was incorporated with F. L Houx, president, Mark Chamberlin treasurer; and George W. Burch, secretary and manager, but E. T. Cheese soon replaced Burch. The blurb ended "Its success is assured".

Now let's see what Agnes Chamberlin recalled. She said, "a very nice, plausible young man by the name of Cheese from Chicago" Talked them into investing in a flour mill. E. T. Cheese, had been a traveling salesman for Marshal Field in Chicago, but probably figured his talents could be better rewarded in another endeavor. He assured a flour mill would make 20% profit on the investment. Mark fell for the deal first and they invested $13,000, borrowing some of the money from the bank. More money had to be sunk in the venture because a storage warehouse had to be built in Greybull and Agnes financed that. The farmers around Cody didn't raise much wheat, what they grew was soft spring wheat, not the best for bread making. Actually most of the wheat was grown and hauled in from Burlington area and from Germainia Bench (now called Emblem). The farmers did not get paid in cash for their wheat but were paid with warehouse receipt that had to be redeemed at the bank. Agnes said the mill ran two years and shut down because the venture failed and she lost $3,500. Investors reopened the mill during the First World War and it ran at a profit for a few months but finally shut down for good.

Photo by Jo Jean DeHony

The big white, three story mill stood as a landmark on the west side if the top of the mill hill, (12th and Wyoming Avenue), for many years and finally a buyer removed the top stories and renovated it into a shop and dwelling. Not much is ever mentioned about this flour mill failure, it was a bad investment every one tried to forget.

Agnes wrote in her memoirs that before she was born her father had gone into partnership with a man in a flour mill in Kansas and lost all his and his wife's money. One wonders why she wasn't more cautious in the Cody flour mill investment.

HIJINKS NEAR THE PAWNEE HOTEL

Observers and bystanders saw this happen in 1958. After the second movie was over in the Cody Theatre on Sheridan Avenue, across from the Irma Hotel, people turned the comer on 12'h Street and drifted home. The clock in the court house had already struck eleven. Suddenly a car shot out of the alley and screeched to a stop in front of the Pawnee Hotel, just as a man in a long trench coat and a slouch hat leaped away from the curb. A loud shot rang out and the man fell to the sidewalk, red blood spreading on his coat and on the sidewalk. Two men jumped out of the car, opened the trunk and stuffed the man in the trunk. Onlookers heard one man shout to the other, "Be sure to get the briefcase!" The car sped away into the dark night.

An observer yelled, "Those guys shot that man in cold blood! Call the sheriff"

No one saw the faces nor got the license plate number. Road blocks were set up, the FBI alerted, and at a high school assembly, law officers asked students to help solve the mystery. Eventually, the excitement died down; upon testing, the blood on the sidewalk did not prove to be human blood.

When the class of 1958 held their 40th reunion in the basement of the Elks Club, one of the graduates took the podium and said, "Finally, after 40 years we can at last tell what happened that night. Some very talented seniors in the drama class staged and directed the episode. I think this was the best kept secret in the history of the school." The four talented drama class students were:

Don Steadman, Jerry Callaway, David Vokac, and Gary Bacon. Thanks to Sandy Pfrangle Holmes for sharing the class secret in 2004.

Do the churches do as much good as the saloons do harm?" Agnes often quoted Emerson, the popular philosopher of the times. William McKinley was President when Mark and Agnes came to Wyoming. After McKinley was assassinated in1901, Theodore Roosevelt took office until 1909; he had strong western ties and was very popular in western States.

She held her own with the business men of Cody and they respected her. She was a "no- nonsense" person, not heavy-set but not the narrow-waisted woman in long skirt photographed in front of the Hart Mountain Inn with fishing catch and dog Dewey in 1901. In later years she wore glasses and dressed in good quality clothing, but nothing flashy.

Agnes Chamberlin
Park County Archives

When she had the first meeting in her home, the Hotel Chamberlin. She belonged to the Cody Club, Eastern Star, and was a charter member of the Cody

Music Club, Playreaders, and Pioneers of the Cody Country. She had been active in organizing the Methodist Church and had helped Reverend Anderson with building plans for the Presbyterian Church. She took an active part in helping The Ladies' Aid Society of the First Presbyterian Church in Cody, in 1909, to compile a 124—page cookbook to raise money for building their church. It was an ecumenical endeavor as more than seventy local ladies submitted recipes. In 1926 she was active in promoting the building of the airport and in 1935, gave her homestead property so the airport could be enlarged.

Agnes Chamberlin holding young goat. c.1918
Photo: Park County Archives

Animals

For about two years she kept chickens, she had goats for a while running up and down elevated planks on the north side of her property. During most of the early years she kept a milking cow, named Lila, in their large barn east of the hotel. Mark milked the cow for her, but she pitched in often when needed. Later she hired a high school boy to do chores. Mark kept his team in the barn for trips to his stone house on Trail Creek, and like other Cody urban barns, after the advent of the automobile, the barn became the garage for the car.

Mark Chamberlin and Dorothy Hiscock, next to the Hotel Chamberlin with his young animals

Agnes Chamberlin and Bingo c.1936
Photo: Park County Archives

It was trendy at the time to keep wild animal pets. After working on the teeth of a road builder, Mark brought a bear cub back from Mormon Creek one time but later Agnes sold it to a zoo in Butte, Montana, but the bear cub from Primm's saloon ran around town freely for awhile, Following their first dog, Dewey, there were numerous other hunting dogs and house dogs. In later years Agnes had a formal photograph taken with her pet of the time sitting on a small table beside her. A photograph of Agnes and dog hangs in one of the booths of the Irma Grill. Another pet that succeeded Dewey had his photograph taken sitting in Agnes' lap' this one they named "Juddy" after Judge Metz who stayed in Hotel Chamberlin when he came up from Basin to handle court cases. Dr. Chamberlin had a hunting dog named "Bobby Bums", that figured in a near-drowning experience of Mark on Beck Lake, related farther on. Agnes at one time had a short haired, white dog named "Bingo" and there may have been others.

Mrs. Rumsey "Anna" Rumsey gave Agnes her green parrot named Loretta. This bird lived in the hotel, but in summer preferred the outdoors. Apparently, it was jointly owned by Agnes and Mable Watson. Traveling salesman taught the parrot naughty words and Jack Hayes, in 2003, remembered when he was a school boy, he liked to hear the parrot swearing as he walked past on his way home to the Depot after school.

Along about August 11, 1938, the thirty-year-old bird disappeared. It had a habit of calling gown a drain pipe and conversing with its echo. A search of the drainpipe and everywhere else failed to find the old bird. An appropriate obituary appeared in the Cody Enterprise.

Hotel

Agnes' sister, Bertha Brown, lived with her for a number of years before Bertha married and moved away in 1912. In 1905 both ladies came into a handsome inheritance and immediately began to consider possible investments. Besides the flour mill, Agnes bought a farm east of Cody and struggled with renters and scanty return until she sold it in 1916, which gave her some hard cash for building her hotel in the spring of 1917.

Her happiness and most successful accomplishment was her hotel. She had gained valuable experience from her boardinghouse. She was financially able at this point to embark on the new venture; she sold a farm east of Cody that she had invested in after receiving an inheritance.

The 28th of March of 1917, she temporarily moved into an empty space across the street in the Walls Building. Her contractors were Algott Johnson and Bill Rankin. They first moved the old frame house to the back and dug a basement in the front for the new hotel. While she and her long time assistant, Mabel Watson, were in the gray sandstone Walls Building they set to work sewing sheets and pillow cases and cotton house dresses.

Mrs Chamberlin in the Lobby of the Hotel Chamberlin

We can get an idea of the lobby from old photographs which show her piano on the east side, on the south side is the wide, well built fireplace with a mounted elk head above it, a small desk and many chairs complete the furnishings. The floor is pictured uncarpeted. The new hotel was barely finished when in 1918, Agnes invested $8,000 in adding more rooms. When she opened her new dining room on the northeast side she had room to seat twenty four at five tables and business boomed because she and Mabel had reputations of being fabulous cooks. She started serving meals on a professional scale when Mabel Watson came to work for her on January 1, 1910, and she closed her popular dining room in 1920 and turned the space into several bedrooms. Another change came when she transformed the old barn into an annex. After World War One came a depression and her business slumped.

Adjacent to Shoshone Reservoir, photo by A. G. Lucier
Courtesy of Wyoming Tales and Trails

Beneath the reservoir's waves are the remnants of the town of Marquette, named after George Marquette. The Town of Marquette was not much. In 1903, it was described as consisting of a few scattered log houses, a little log post office and a school-house described as "a little log structure, crude, bare, unattractive, but occupying a lightly sheltered pot on the South Fork of the Shoshone River." Slightly downstream from the town was a wire cable structure stretched from post to post on either side of the river. Suspended from the cable was a small box, attached to a rope and pulley attachments by means of which the occupant of the box could pull himself across the river during periods of high water. Marquette had come to the South Fork of the Stinking Water in 1881 and in 1882 established a ranch at what is now the site of the reservoir. George Marquette received his first land patent in 1891. The town received its post office in 1890.

As justice of the peace and acting coroner, Marquette investigated the killing in 1892 of the horse thief John M. "Jack" Bliss along the South Fork in an area now known as "Bliss Meadows." Bliss was killed by a former partner in crime, Alfred "Slick" Nard, reputedly a former member of the Hole-in-the-Wall gang. [Writer's note: Nard' first name is sometimes also referred to as "Albert."] Slick had such an awful reputation that when he was taken into custody for the shooting of William Ewing near present-day Slick Creek ["Creek" is pronounced "Crick"], the deputies sneaked him out of Thermopolis in the dark of the night in order to preclude him from being freed by the other outlaws. Ed Farlow recalled:

> In the morning there was a little excitement when I came over to dress Ewing's wounds. Slick and the deputies were gone and no one knew just how. Several of the boys were at the saloon talking about it. When I rode up they told me Slick had gone.
>
> I said, "Yes, I know it. He should be on the top of Ten Sleep Mountain now on his way to Buffalo."
>
> Mike Brown spoke up and asked what was the big idea.
>
> I told him straight. "We did not know how soon you fellows would say 'turn him loose.'" Mike replied, "Turn that son of a bitch loose? If you had said the word we would have helped you hang him. I want you to know this, Farlow. We may rob a bank, or hold up a stage or a railroad pay car now and then, but we are not killing working men for their money. We are not that damn low yet." **Farlow, Edward J, *Wind River Adventure*, High Plains Press, Glendo, 1998.**

Nard was married to Jennie Hollywood, sister of Thermopolis saloonist John "Jack" Hollywood. Hollywood himself was reputed to have killed three men, but convicted only once, and that for manslaughter of Smith Bray in 1909. Hollywood's defense was three-fold: (a) His shooting of Bray didn't really kill Bray; Bray died of hypostatic pneumonia caused by a weakened heart brought on by the use of morphine. (b) Self-defense. (c) Bray had forgiven him. On Bray's deathbed when Bray was "feeling badly," Bray told a nurse, "It is no use. I am going to die in spite of hell. I want to tell you Jack was not to blame. It was all my fault."

Allegedly, Marquette was unable to find any friends of Bliss along the South Fork, and directed that Bliss be buried on the spot along the Stinking Water where Bliss fell. Bliss's bones were later swept away in a flood.

Workers on the Shonshone Dam, 1908
Courtesy of Wyoming Tales and Trails

But the death of Bliss was not the only one with which Marquette was indirectly involved. Marquette was noted for his ability with a fiddle and would thus play at dances. Dances were a popular entertainment in the 1880's. People would travel miles to a dance. In the 1880's, the only town around with a hall was Arland located near present day Meeteetse. Arland was not much of a town, consisting of the obligatory saloon, livery stable, and store operated by the town's founders John F. Corbett (1848-1910) and Victor Arland. Corbett was originally from Massachusetts and Arland from France. The town also had a hotel or rooming house, the rooms of which were separated by "walls" made of muslin sheets. Rose Williams operated a sporting parlor. Corbett and Arland had come to the area about 1880 from Ft. Custer and established a trading post near the foot of Rattlesnake Mountain near present day Cody. In 1883, the two moved the trading post to Cottonwood Creek. At Ft. Custer, Corbett had been a freighter and Arland had, apparently, been a buffalo hunter and earlier a miner in the Black Hills. In 1883, the wagon road from Rawlins to Red Lodge, Montana, had been established by the government and the businessmen of Red Lodge had raised a public subscription to build a $5,000.00 bridge across the Stinking Water. Thus, the following year Corbett and Arland moved the trading post once again, apparently to be closer to the action produced by the twice-a-week stage. Thus, the town of Arland was born.

In 1887, Marquette was providing the fiddle music for a dance at the Hall in Arland. On the night in question, Marquette was tuning up and the dancers pairing up. There appeared in the doorway an individual variously known as "Broken Nose" Jackson or "Rawhide" Jackson. The music stopped. A hush came over the crowd, that strange silence which occurs when there is some horrible faux pas. There lying on the doorstep was the dead body of Jackson and in Victor Arland's hand was a smoking gun. The festivities, however, resumed, with Vic's remonstrance, "Stop staring like a bunch of idiots. Start up the music, he can't hurt you. He's dead." Jackson was stowed away in a backroom awaiting burial the next day. And as old-fashioned social columns used to say, "A good time was had by all." Three years later, Vic Arland and Rose Williams were visiting Red Lodge. While Vic was playing poker in Dunivan's Saloon, he was killed by a shot through the window. Rose Williams, herself, was ultimately found dead in the road outside of a house belonging to Belle Drewry about five miles downstream from Arland.

The music finally stopped in Arland in 1897. At a dance, Belle Drewry plugged Jesse Conway. Belle was, as they say, "a professional lady" and had arrived in Arland about 1891 from Sundance where she had run into problems with the law. Conway and Corbett were in a dispute over the affections of Belle. Earlier, others found themselves pushing up daisies as a result of such disputes. William Gallagher, a Pitchfork cowboy, was killed by Bill Wheaton after Gallagher beat up Belle. Previously, Belle and Gallagher had been friends. When Bill was arrested for improperly branding a horse, Belle had gone his bail. A one-eyed cowboy named Bill Hoolihan attempted to avenge Gallagher's killing. Wheaton was the better shot. Wheaton was sent off to Laramie for eight years.

After Conway was plugged, his friends loaded his body over the back of a horse and departed. The next day, however, they returned and killed Belle and three of her co-workers. By this time, Meeteetse had been founded and probably the main *raison d'etre* for the continued viability of Arland were the ladies. With their deaths, Arland faded from existence, the only trace remaining is the cemetery.

Cody, Wyoming, approx. 1910
Courtesy of Wyoming Tales and Trails

Cody was platted in 1895 by Beck and Alger, with whom William F. Cody joined after learning of the proposed development from his son-in-law, Horton Boal (1865-1902), one of the surveyors for the project. The first building was constructed in 1896. Thus, Cody celebrates its founding as 1896. By 1901 the Cody Club, an ancestor of the Chamber of Commerce, was formed. Boal was the husband of Cody's oldest daughter Arta. Both Beck and Alger had run for governor on the Democrat slate and had been defeated. Beck was first bypassed by President Cleveland for territorial governor, when Cleveland appointed Thomas Moonlight of Kansas. Beck was then defeated in a race for Congress in 1890 and was again lost a race for governor in 1902. Alger, a banker, served as mayor of Sheridan in 1889, but was defeated in the race for governor in 1898.

Originally, Cody proposed to locate the town at the Springs, but eventually the town was located about a mile downstream. DeMaris Springs were named after Charles DeMaris who homesteaded in the area in the late 1880's and proved up his homestead in 1894. It was also proposed to call the town "Shoshone." The name, however, was rejected by the Post Office because of possible confusion with Shoshoni.

PICTURES AND CAPTIONS TAKEN FROM WYOMING TALES AND TRAILS

Cody, looking northwest, approx. 1910.
Courtesy of Wyoming Tales and Trails

A history of an area is often found in its street names. This is true of Cody. In addition to Gerrans, Bleistein and Rumsey Avenues, the town's founders, George T. Beck and Horace Alger are commerated in the names of streets. Another street is named after the Wild West show's general manager, Nate Salsbury. Although there is an Ingraham Dr., it was not named after the show's advance agent, Prentise Ingraham (1843-1904). Instead Ingraham Dr. and Newton Ave. are named after early settlers in Park County.

Sheridan Ave., looking east, Cody, Approx. 1910
Courtesy of Wyoming Tales and Trails

The above photo was taken from in front of the Irma Hotel.

Hauling Wool, Cody, Wyoming.

Wool Train, Sheridan Ave., 1908.
Courtesy of Wyoming Tales and Trails

Although, William F. Cody certainly had in mind tourism to Yellowstone, the primary purpose of the founding of the Town of Cody was agricultural to take advantage of irrigation and the Carey Act. For discussion of the Carey Act, see Laramie. Indeed, the project was one of the first Carey Act developments in the State. The project was promoted in the Wild West Show. As observed by one of his partners, George Beck, Cody was "the best advertised man in America." But as long the Wild West show business manager Nate Salsbury was alive, some control over the flow of money was maintained. In 1902, Salsbury died and Cody's investments began to grow. By 1905, Cody's Shoshone Land and Irrigation Company had some 6,500 acres under irrigation. Settlers remained few and far between, but the lawsuits flowed like water, with some twenty-six suits filed against the Company. Today, the project is regarded as one of the most successful reclamation developments, but it never made money.

Following Cody's death in 1917, plans for a proper memorial in Cody began. As noted earlier, Cody had the misfortune to die in Denver, permitting the residents of that State to memorialize him with a grave on Lookout Mountain west of Denver rather than on Cedar Mountain overlooking his namesake city. Nevertheless, on February 19, 1917, the Legislature appropriated $5,000 to be used for a memorial. By March the Buffalo Bill Memorial Association was organized which received contributions from local citizens as well as large contributions from Cornlius Vanderbilt and Rodman Wanamaker. Fifty-five acres of land was acquired adjoining the town and on July 4, 1924 an equestrian statute costing $35,000 was dedicated.

Shoshone Dam and Reservoir, photos
by A. G. Lucier, Left photo, 1924, Right, 1926,
Cody Road to right in photos.
Courtesy of Wyoming Tales and Trails

In 1895, 1897, and 1899, Wm. F. Cody and Nate Salsbury (1846-1902) acquired the right to take water from the Stinking Water as a part of his plans for the Shoshone Land and Irrigation Company. Financially strapped, Cody ultimately turned to the Federal Government to take over the project. Salsbury was partner with Cody in the Wild West Show and was general manager. To him some give credit for Cody's success, and attribute Cody's subsequent problems to the fact that after Salsbury's death, Cody no longer had anyone to manage his affairs and keep him away from women, liquor, and bad investments. It should be noted, however, that in the last years of his life, Cody was a teetotaler.

Spillway, Shoshone Dam, approx. 1935.
Photo by A. G. Lucier courtesy of Betty Amundson
Courtesy of Wyoming Tales and Trails

The bus is a White. In 1903, the government took over the project. The following year, the State Engineer, Clarence T. Johnson, reported that the Reservoir when completed would permit the irrigation of 200,000 acres of arid land. Construction of the dam started in 1905, but the first contractor soon abandoned the job. Difficulties encountered included no ready source of sand or gravel for the concrete and problems when 1/2 of the entire annual flow of the Shoshone River came in one thirty-day period. A second contractor took over the work in 1906. The same year, the Reclamation Service was required to take over the construction of the Corbett Tunnel portion of the job. When the dam was completed in 1910, it was the highest concrete arch dam in the world, with a height of 325 feet, a thickness of 108 feet at its base, and a width of 200 feet across. The Reservor and Dam were renamed after Buffalo Bill 1946. By 1975, the reservoir provided irrigation to about half of the original expectation, 94,000 acres. Additionally, the dam provides power through the 5,600 kilowatt power plant. Today, the project is regarded as one of the most successful reclamation developments, but it never made money.

After Mark died in 1922, Dr. Moody rented Dr. Chamberlin's office and practiced in Cody for a number of years. Dr. Moody played in Cody bands and lived at the corner of 9th and Rumsey Avenue. By the early 1930's she must have already added the rooms above Dr. Chamberlin's dental offices as appear in a photograph from the 1930's. The big, open, covered porch on the west side of the second story provided a space for people to wait for the Yellowstone Park buses. Ed Hunter, in March of 2003, remembered as a youngster, he picked up the Billings Gazette at the Chamberlin Hotel bus stop when he delivered papers.

Cody Cowboy Band. Photo by F. J. Hiscock.
Courtesy of Wyoming Tales and Trails

If the novel's central villainess, the Lady Doc, Dr. Emma Harpe, was taken to be Dr. Lane, Miss Lockhart wrote with a heavy hand. The central character Dr. Harpe was drawn as an incompetent, greedy money grubbing abortionist, who was forced to leave Nebraska under threat of losing her medical license for killing a patient in a forbidden operation. Dr. Harpe was depicted as one who stole from patients while they were under ether. The efforts of George Beck to bring irrigation to the Basin were unmercifully grilled. Miss Lockhart depicted the prospective purchasers of new farms coming to see "the land 'where the perfumed zephyrs fanned the cheeks of men and brothers!' Coming to breathe 'the Elixir of Life,' • while they inspected that portion of the desert which was 'blooming like the rose!'" as arriving in a dust storm:

RELIGION

CHRISTIAN SCIENCE PLAYED an increasingly big role in Agnes' life as she got more and more involved in it. It had intrigued her for a long time before she started reading its doctrines, which she became more interested in about 1913. A great many of the early Cody ladies were Christian Scientists. Agnes stated Mrs. Calkins was the first Christian Scientist she knew of in Cody. Mr. Calkins was editor of the Cody Enterprise and came here from Lusk where he founded the Lusk newspaper and he had been in the newspaper business in Casper. Other early Scientists were Mrs. Tinkcom; Mrs. Van Horn; Mrs. Oskins; Mrs. Watkins, Mrs. Beck, Mrs. Parks and Mrs. Tex Holms in whose house the meetings were first held. Mrs. Eldred and Mrs. Hutsonpillar were "practitioners". From Mrs. Holms living room they moved to the back room of the Masonic Temple, then to the basement of the Carnegie Library where they stayed until they built the red brick building on the corner of Sheridan Avenue and 9th Street. The sale of the Orchard's house on Canyon Avenue provided most of the money to build the Christian Science church. Young Thorton Beck, played tennis with Don Flora and alerted him of the availability of the Orchard house which the Floras bought.

In 2003 Pat Helmbolt and Ruth Sperry remembered as little girls of Brooks and Huldah Borron they attended Christian Science Sunday school, they particularly enjoyed and recalled their teachers wore fashionable dresses and elegant perfumes and Mrs. Chamberlin was a very sweet person. Huldah Borron's Swedish family was Lutheran but Cody had no Lutheran church and Huldah worked for a lady whose Christian Science faith was compelling. Pat has had many medical problems for which she needed medical doctors but has stayed with Christian Science. Ruth embraced Catholicism. By 2003 only a handful of Christian Scientists attended the Cody church.

Agnes went to Denver to study Christian Science under a Mr. Rathvon and met his student Clyde Johnson a practitioner from Sheridan. Agnes said she had an itching of her scalp which was cured by Clyde. Agnes showed her gratitude by sending him monthly checks in the 1933 era and gave him $500 towards a new car. To quote Agnes, "This true and understanding friendship is one of the best things that has come into my life and brought physical and mental healing. Clyde has raised my opinion of myself and showed me I was a better woman than I thought I was and have a better standing in the community".

Altamae Markham, in 2003, recalled Mrs. Chamberlin had a goiter because Mrs. Markham also had a goiter which she had surgically removed in 1919, the treatment for this fairly common ailment of the times. Later iodized salt cut the incidence of goiter. Agnes did not mention her goiter in her memoirs. According to Agnes' death certificate she died of a coronary occlusion due to her goiter, or as the certificate says, the goiter was an antecedent cause. Apparently, loyal to her beliefs, she refused medical treatment.

(THE FOLLOWING QUOTES FROM ANNE'S ARCHIVES, WILL REPEAT MANY OF THE PREVIOUS ITEMS MENTIONED IN THE ACTUAL WRITINGS BY AGNES CHAMBERLIN, BUT WILL BE REPEATED AS THE INFORMATION MAY EXTEND FROM THE PREVIOUS WRITINGS)

AGNES CHAMBERLIN

Quotes from Anne's Archives (Anne Fendrich)

Anne says, "For the past two weeks I have been quoting from a manuscript written by the late Agnes B. Chamberlin, and I thought you would like to know more about this Cody Pioneer, as I did. I found a copy of her obituary in a January, 1949 Cody Enterprise." Mrs. Chamberlin had passed away on January 17, 1949, just three days before her 78th birthday.

Agnes Virginia Brown had been born in New Milford, Illinois on January 20, 1871. Her education in Peabody, Kansas included the study of business. On February 6, 1899 she married Dr. Mark Chamberlin, and the two lived for a short time in Wheatland, Wyoming. They moved to Cody in 1900. She owned and operated the Chamberlin Hotel (Pawnee Hotel) for many years until her retirement in 1939. She was secretary of the Cody Club for years and wrote a history of that organization. She was the first president of the Buffalo Bill Memorial Association. In fact, she called the first meeting at her home in the autumn of 1926 to promote the idea of a museum building.

Dedication for the museum was held July 4, 1927. Agnes Chamberlin was a pianist and a charter member of the Cody Music Club. She was also a charter member of the Play readers. She was a charter member of the Pioneers of the Cody Country and a member of the board of trustees of that organization.

She was a supporter of our local churches. According to Melissa Winter, Mrs. Chamberlin had been her minister-father's right arm during the building of the first Presbyterian Church in Cody. She also had been active in the Methodist Church. She organized the Christian Science Church in Cody.

In 1927, the railroad by-passed Cody's hotels and constructed the Burlington Inn.
Courtesy of Wyoming Tales and Trails

JO JEAN THOMAS DEHONY

Burlington Inn 1930's
Courtesy of Wyoming Tales and Trails

The Burlington Inn had 90 rooms. The dining room could hold 400 to 500 persons. The Inn only operated seasonally when the road to Yellowstone was open. It's back bar is now on display in the Meeteetse Museum. Before World War II, the tourists arrived by train, traveled up the Cody Road to Yellowstone and when they returned they stayed at the Burlington Inn. As many as 50 busses would wait for the arrival of a train to take the tourists to Yellowstone.

When the Cody Airport was planned in 1928, she was influential in its promotion, and she gave her homestead to Cody in 1935 so the airport could be enlarged and "to assure its location on this side of the river". This dynamic woman must have been a well-loved and respected member of our community. On the day of her funeral, Mayor Hugh Smith ordered all businesses closed so that all might attend it.

According to Mrs. Winter, Agnes Chamberlin is another one who has not received the recognition she deserves form our community. Just recently, in observance of National Library Week, Mr. and Mrs. J. C., Gilbert donated five flower panels to the Park Co Library. Each panel honors the memory of an outstanding Cody woman. Among those so honored are Mrs. Mary Jester Allen, Mrs. Maud Murray, Miss Margery Ross, Mrs. Jessie Walters and Mrs. Agnes B. Chamberlin.

Mark

Mark Chamberlin figures as an antagonist in Agnes' diary. They seemed quite compatible the first few years but after nineteen years of marriages she moved him out of her bedroom when she built the main hotel in 1917. He seemed to adjust to this and threw himself into his work, recreation and his own interests for the following five years before he died. Agnes disliked it when Mark went off hunting or traipsing in the mountains. She said he would take off hunting for a few days and stay away weeks and she had to make excuses to his patients, she felt he should buckle down and keep his nose to the grindstone.

Mark Chamberlin was Cody's first dentist and there seem to be no allusions to any malpractice. He succeeded in his practice and built his own brick office. Caroline Lockhart mentions in her diary about seeing Doc Chamberlin about a tooth. **In** Lucille Patrick's, *Caroline Lockhart, Liberated Lady—1870-1963,* Lucille quotes from Caroline's diary that in February of 1919, Caroline questions Mark for news (and gossip) about Bill Miller, (the Italian Count deColona who went to World War I with the Big Horn Basin, Company K, returned wounded and a hero). Caroline had a crush on Bill and it made her very jealous if Bill sparked some other woman. She felt she could depend on Mark for reliable information.

HISTORIC CABIN -- members of the Historical Society also visited this historic spot and inspected the cabin built over 50 years ago by Dr. and Mrs. Chamberlain on Trail Creek.

Park County Historical Archives

JO JEAN THOMAS DEHONY

He bought a homestead relinquishment up Trail Creek and built into the side hill a two room stone house that still stands ninety years later. He had only flood water rights for irrigating his pastureland, not a reliable source, but he loved the place and Agnes hated it. He kept a team and wagon and drove out there every weekend. Park County Archives holds a letter written in 1921 by Mark Chamberlin, the year before his death, in which he invited friends to visit and enjoy his summer cabin. Agnes wrote she didn't care to cope with the property after Mark's death so she made a deal with Harry Sanborn and he assumed the place and its debts.

Mark wanted to be a successful hunter and sportsman but from Agnes' writings we get a picture of a sincere but rather inept man. While fishing on Beck Lake his boat capsized, He and his two dogs were thrown in the water and he nearly drowned because one dog kept climbing on top of his head forcing his head under the water.

Their first winter in Cody there was no meat market, Mark shot an elk for winter meat, but they did not know how to properly cool and hang it and blow flies destroyed it. Years later, when trying to entertain at a party by standing on his head he fell and crashed into something. He was into healthful exercise by working out on two large rings suspended in his bedroom. It was considered humorous that once he nearly strangled by getting tangled up in the leather straps holding the rings.

On the positive he neither caroused nor drank nor womanized. He served as a councilman on first Cody town councils. He persevered in the Masonic order and played chess with other serious minded men. He pursued his profession by taking courses and reading his professional journals. According to Cody city council minutes, on June 17, 1903, J. W. Chapman applied for a county liquor license. Mark Chamberlain protested about the rowdiness of Chapman's saloon near the Chamberlain residence and Chapman's application was rejected. The Chamberlin's soon moved off Sheridan Avenue, around the corner to 12th Street and Chapman eventually got his license.

The most important community organizations, however, are those devoted to the Buffalo Bill Museum and to the Cody Stampede and the Cody Nite Rodeo.

Bob Crisp Coming Off Crumbling Ann, Cody Stampede,
photo by Ralph Doubleday, see text below.
Courtesy of Wyoming Tales and Trails

Cody Stampede Parade, approx. 1930, photo by F. J. Hiscock
Courtesy of Wyoming Tales and Trails

The Stampede was started in 1918 in an effort to attract tourists to the area and was timed in June in that year so as to predate the advent of Prohibition. As indicated by the next photo, there had, of course, been rodeos before the war. The Stampede's first president was local newspaper woman and novelist Caroline Cameron Lockhart (1871-1962). Miss

Lockhart came to Cody in 1904 after having worked for the *Boston Post* and the *Philadelphia Bulletin.*

Carl Downing in Bucking Contest, 1909. Photo by F. J. Hiscock.
Courtesy of Wyoming Tales and Trails

F. J. Hiscock, "The Picture Man," undated
Park County Archives

Carl "Carly" Downing later appeared with his older brother Gailord "Gail" Downing in Col. Cody's Wild West show. Carl Downing was also a founder of the Stampede and helped organize the Cody Nite Rodeo in 1938. Other members of the Wild West settled in Cody. Among them was Frank N. Hammitt (1870-1903) who appeared in an early 1894 Edison movie, filmed in Brooklyn when the Wild West was playing in New York. The film shows another "real" cowboy, Lee Martin, riding his bronco Sunfish while Hammitt standing on the corral fence fires a gun. Originally Hammitt, Chief of the Cowboys in the show, was also to ride his horse El Dorado but the little studio did not have room. Hammitt moved to Cody in 1898 and became a ranger in the Yellowstone Forest Reserve. He was killed when he fell from a cliff in 1903.

Joseph Jesse Faver "Fay Jay" Hiscock (F. J. Hiscock) (1874-1951), many of whose pictures are featured on these pages, was originally from Kalamazoo, Michigan. He remained active in photography in Cody from his arrival in 1904 until the early 1940's, and sold packages of photographs to tourists. The packages were primarily of the Cody Road. In his advertising he referred to himself as "The Picture Man."

Agnes wrote that Mark went back to Chicago in 1906 for a postgraduate course in dentistry. The fact that he never graduated probably bothered Agnes more than it did Mark. However, although the dental school he had attended about a decade previously no longer existed, Mark located a man who had been an official and who still had some school diplomas. For $50.00 the man filled out the form for Mark and he returned to Cody with an impressive diploma. And he did upgrade by taking some courses. Agnes said he also kept up by reading dental journals, and she did admit "he made good".

The first Masonic Lodge was started in Meeteetse and Mark Chamberlin joined that group and took his First Degree and persevered to reach the Thirty First Degree with the Cody Lodge. Agnes dutifully joined Eastern Star, Cedar Chapter No. 14 in 1908, and they benefited from her musical ability. She said she belonged until about 1935, but never cared much for it.

Mark did show courage during the November 1904 bank holdup across 12th Street of the First National Bank by two masked men. Mark grabbed his .40-.65 caliber pistol and ran out to take a shot at the bandits. However, in fumbling to insert the shells, it was too late to get a good shot. It is interesting to note that after the holdup citizens were advised to keep their guns loaded and ready for action. I. O. Middaugh, bank cashier, was murdered, and despite a $500 reward the bandits were never apprehended. It is interesting to note that two previous holdups were never solved.

On December 23, 1902 two masked men held up Ben Primm's saloon, and in October of 1904, "two masked and armed men held up R. A. Roth's saloon, carrying off more than $400. Their horses were tied behind the Cody Drug building."

Park County Archives

According to Mark Chamberlin's death certificate he died in Dr. Whitlock's Powell Hospital on August 17, 1922, of sarcoma. Dr. Whitlock admitted him to his hospital on July 20th and he died 28 days later and was buried at Riverside Cemetery where later faithful Mabel Watson date> and Agnes were buried. (Agnes bought this plot in (2005, there are still three unused spaces in the Chamberlin plot. The nine used spaces are Mark and Agnes Chamberlin: Walter d. Sanzenbocker. 1881-1980, and his two wives, Pauline, 1877-1924, and Dorothea; Juanita Miller Lens, 1885-1945, and Ferdinand Lens O'Aubigne, a destitute French Count, 1868-1947, Mabel Watson, 1885-1939, Agnes' faithful helper; and Robert A.Blair 1860-1942, hotel handyman)

In 1913 two Swedish immigrant sisters, Hulda and Ester Nilson, worked for Mr. and Mrs. B. C. Rumsey at their Dairy Ranch on the bench south of Cody and north-east of Beck Lake. On July 25, 1913, Ester Nilson suffered a toothache. According to her diary, which she wrote in Swedish, she caught a ride to Cody with Mrs. Eli (Mattie) Jernberg and visited the dentist-Dr. Chamberlin. On July 29th she had to return to Dr. Chamberlin "for a filling which took two hours and cost ten dollars". She had no further trouble. Ester Nilson was the aunt of Ester Johansson Murray the researcher of this paper.

The fact that Mark Chamberlin was Cody's first dentist which he carried out in a creditable manner should give him a notable place in Cody's history.

Caroline Lockhart, 1920. Photo by F. J. Hiscock.

Caroline Lockhart
Courtesy of Wyoming Tales and Trails

JO JEAN THOMAS DEHONY

Prior to becoming a newspaper writer and after attendance at the "Monrovian Seminary for Young Ladies," Miss Lockhart appeared on the stage and in a lion taming act in a circus. She actually entered the lion's cage the day after the lion killed her predecessor. As a newspaper writer, she donned diving gear to go to the bottom of Boston Harbor and jumped four floors to test the Boston Fire Department safety net. Among her novels were *Me-Smith* and *The Lady Doc*.

The Lady Doc in its depiction of the fictional town of "Crowheart" was well received nationally, but in Cody the novel was greeted with a degree of frostiness which might remind one of those clear chilling winds which blow out of the northwest on a January morning. Indeed, Miss Lockhart's books were removed from the shelves in the library. Miss Lockhart responded with a salvo against one of the members of the Library Board. Miss Lockhart wrote that the member was "one of those women who could go anywhere in the world without fear of molestation from the opposite sex."

The general nastiness continued until in 1922 it boiled over into an issue as to the future direction of the Stampede with Lockhart accusing some of wanting to turn it into a Chautaugua.

The characters in *Lady Doc* were regarded as depictions of well-known Cody residents including George Beck, Daisy Beck, Bronson Rumsey, Jake Schwoob manager of the Cody Trading Company, and the town's physician Dr. Frances Margaret Lane. Dr. Lane had arrived in Cody in 1902 and had a contract with the federal government to provide certain medical services. Later, Dr. Lane would be the Chairman of the Wyoming Branch of the National Woman's Party.

We all enjoy seeing the foibles of the well-known being exaggerated and satirized. That is the essence of a good roast, but *The Lady Doc* perhaps went too far. No one was safe. Not even Cody's Cowboy Band. Miss Lockhart wrote of the Band as:

> *** a conflict of sounds which resembled the efforts of a Chinese orchestra *** making superhuman endeavors to march and yet produce a sufficiently correct number of notes from the score of "A Hot Time in the Old Town" to make that American war cry recognizable ***"

COMMUNITY STANDING AND SOCIAL LIFE

Before her big hotel kept her busy she entered into the social life of Cody, she and Mark entertained and were entertained as a couple at card parties, chafing dish suppers, and dances.

Agnes also took an active part in plays, also providing piano music for all sorts of programs, and guided the women's club from 1905 to 1910. Along with her memoirs are her notes of nineteen pages of suggestions for club discussions. Some of her questions were: "Do you think we are having a harder time pioneering in Wyoming than our Parents had in our native states? What do you consider?

The worst drawback to Cody, the moral atmosphere or the high wind? Are the women of Cody using their ballots to the best interests of the community?" Agnes was much in demand as an accompanist for Miss Calkins and Mr. Hey, violinists, and for dances. She played pieces such as "Tarantelle" and "Because" at local concerts. She played for Eastern Star functions and later for the Christian Science church. Her solid music foundation at Kansas State University prepared her well.

In the 1910 election the northern part of Big Horn County decided to form their own county which they named "Park". One of their name choices was "Beck" after George T. Beck, which would have been a proper memorial to an entrepreneur who guided and directed the government and the economy of this area so beneficially. Before the county court house was planned and built Park County government was housed in a one-story brick building on the northeast corner of the Chamberlain property. A photograph taken of the ten newly elected county officers and Colonel W. F. Cody standing on the east end of the group was taken in front of the temporary brick "court house".

Buffalo Bill Cody stands next to the first Park County officials elected in November of 1910. Left to Right, Henry Fulkerson—Assessor, Andy Martin—Commissioner, Henry Dahlem—Sheriff, Walter Kepford—Commissioner, Jessie Hitchcock—Superintendent of Schools, W. H. Fouse—Commissioner, Gus Holm—Treasurer, F. M. Cowell—Deputy Clerk, and Fred Barnett—Clerk.

In 1975 Jo Jean DeHony pointed out evidence of the foundation of the steel vault used at the time. Later a second story and gambrel roof were added to the brick building and it was stuccoes on the outside. What financial arrangement between the Chamberlains and Park County in regard to this structure is at this time not known?

Agnes had a good standing in the community. Two things might be mentioned that elevated Agnes' standing in the community. One is an unsolicited act of kindness recounted by Doneness Kant Kaufman in March of 2003. Back in the 1940's, Charlotte, "Kay" Kant, a single mother of two children owned the K and K clothing store. She also rented a log house on 8th Street owned by Ray Horton, Boilermaker and plumber, who lived in the basement. The Horton's decided to move to California and needed to sell their house immediately for cash. Kay was making payments on a car and the bank would not loan her any money. She didn't feel she could move and the situation seemed bleak causing many tears. Mrs. Chamberlain came into the store, sympathized with the unhappy mother and calmed her down saying "things will work out alright". Mrs. Chamberlain then went to the bank and subsidized a loan, which Kay could pay off at $50.00 or more a month, which she did. When the loan was paid, Kay sent Mrs. Chamberlin a dozen roses to which she replied she had made many loans over the years and this was the first act of appreciation she had ever received.

Sheridan Ave., approx. 1940, photo by F. J. Hiscock
Courtesy of Wyoming Tales and Trails

A contribution that gives Agnes Chamberlain a lasting place in the history of Cody is Her compilation of *The Story of The Cody Club 1900-1940,*. This was printed by J. T. Little. June Little of New York and Cody. Breck Moran, then editor of The *Cody Enterprise* helped edit the manuscript. The sixty three pages were carefully assembled and researched by Agnes. The forest green cover bears a photograph on the front of Colonel Cody at his TE ranch with his white horse, Isham. Agnes qualified for writing up the history of The Cody Club, as she had been a faithful secretary of the club for many years.

Other volunteer positions she held: very noteworthy is the fact she was elected the first President of the Buffalo Bill Memorial Association in 1926, when she hosted the first meeting in her home at the Hotel. She was a Charter Member of the following organizations: Cody Music Club: Play readers; and Pioneers of the Cody Country. She had been active in organizing the Methodist Church and helped Reverend Anderson with building plans for the Presbyterian Church. In 1928 she was active in promoting the building of the airport and in 1935, gave her homestead property so the airport could be enlarged.

Agnes Chamberlain, along with four other early Cody women, is memorialized by one of five Famed panels of original wild flower paintings by Elizabeth Gilbert, that hang in the Park County Library reading room. Panel number IV is dedicated to Agnes Brown Chamberlain, 1871-1947.

JO JEAN THOMAS DEHONY

The short narrative includes the fact she arrived in 1900 by wagon, bringing along her sewing machine, and lived to help dedicate KODI radio station in 1947. The eight wildflowers in her panel include purple gentians, shooting stars, and bluebells.

THE FOLLOWING IS AGAIN ACTUAL WRITINGS BY: Agnes Chamberlin AND MAY BE REPEATED INFORMATION) (each article contains a little different and more complete information.)

AGNES CHAMBERLIN

"The building of the hotel in 1917 separated Mark an me for good as far as having anything in common went," wrote Agnes in her 1936 memoirs. Back in 1898, Agnes met Mark Chamberlin in Woodward Oklahoma, where he was a practicing dentist, albeit unlicensed, and she worked ten hours a day for $6.00 a week in a print shop. On February 6, 1899, twenty-eight year old Agnes married thirty-five year old Mark in Peabody, Kansas. When she met Mark in Woodward her friends urged her to marry him for "security". In her memoirs she wrote, "with grave doubts and a heavy heart" she went forward with preparations for her marriage, and she tried to content her-self with second best. However, the marriage at her parent's home in Kansas went well, and, despite the fact she had no dowry, they set up house-keeping in a compatible manner in Woodward.

Unfortunately, Mark had been practicing without a license, and, when put on the spot, he did not pass his state dental examination and was forced to leave town and seek in another state. Agnes stayed behind suffering the humiliation from insinuations and gossip that Mark had deserted her. This is one of the times in her memoirs she mentioned that she wished she had embraced Christian Science at the time.

Back to Agnes' story in 1900

There was a point in time they seemed to need each other, and she wrote that Mark was very kind and she felt great loyalty to him during his adversities. Soon patients needing a dentist in Hartville and Guernsey petered out, and they must set out again. Mark bought a wagon and team, a bay and a grey, from a rancher who threw into the deal, his dog, Dewey, a speckled, black and white, short-haired pointer. Mark fitted up the wagon, sheep wagon style, so they could travel and live in it, and they set off towards Thermopolis, in the northern part of the State. The high plains area of what is now Platte County, Wyoming, is bountiful habitat for the western meadow lark. Its melodic song and bright yellow feathers must have cheered them along their way. They probably followed a wagon road close to the route of the California-Oregon Trail from Guernsey to Casper, except for their excursion around the sharp, blue landmark of Laramie Peak. During these early years. With a population of only 92,531 in 1900, Wyoming offered plenty of wide open, uncluttered space. Mark reveled in it; Agnes endured it.

Agnes wrote that they got along well when they were first married. She called him Hubby in her early diary. He enjoyed the fishing and hunting, and had hopes of shooting a deer, as they traveled around the west side of Laramie peak and she put up with the hardships of camping. "No doubt, their sleep was disturbed some nights by the restless snorting of the horses and the smarting smell of a passing skunk. Without light, night skies glowed with starry skies, no air pollution sullied the atmosphere, and every high spot provided hundreds of miles of clear vision with sharp views from one mountain range to another"

They stayed a week in Glenrock where mark picked up a little work and Agnes learned the story of their dog Dewey, a speckled, short hair pointer, apparently well bred but untrained. It began with a family named Thompson, who ran a small hotel. One of their married daughters was Mrs. Barker, whose husband was Dewey's former owner. This is the story of Dewey before the Chamberlin's became the owner of the dog. Near Glenrock there were several sheep raisers and the town dogs began to harass the flocks. The owner of one flock of sheep told Barker that if he ever caught Dewey in his sheep pens he would shoot him and eventually Dewey was caught ham stringing the sheep and the owner peppered Dewey with "bird shot", not really doing any serious damage except to barkers temper. The next time Barker encountered the sheep man he gave him a thrashing. The same night someone shot Barker through a window at his home, killing him at once. The sheep man was tried for murder but because there was only circumstantial evidence he was acquitted. Mrs. Barker did not want to keep the dog so she gave him to Connally, Marks rancher friend, from whom Mark bought his team wagon with the dog included.

Mark and Agnes had no children and Dewey acted like their rowdy, undisciplined teenager. He loved to go hunting and would beg first one and then the other while running to the hunting clothes and gear hanging in the corner and would go wild with joy when one of them gave in to take him out.

The dog went along to Cody and figured in all they did until after a couple years in Cody it was poisoned. This must have been disturbing to everyone because in the records of the city council meeting for March 9, 1904, George

T. Beck, prominent founder of Cody, petitioned the council to make it a crime and a misdemeanor to poison dogs. Agnes Wrote that when he passed away they both grieved. Agnes said, "I put his body in a gunny sack and carried him by horseback down by the river and buried him."

Returning to the Chamberlin's trip, after a week in Glenrock they resumed their trek across the state. Drinking water proved no problem as most sources were potable, except where alkali warned them by its grainy white deposits and foul smell. Their slow progress northward across Wyoming gave time for adventures and encounters with colorful pioneers. Finding no incentive for a dentist in Casper they headed their wagon north on the Bridger Trail.

Jim Bridger guided emigrant travelers on this western route which he chose to avoid trespassing on Sioux territory east of the Big Horn Mountains. This trail also served as an alternate route to the Bozeman Trail. Bridger's trail started on the Platte River crossing at Casper, then turned west and northwest to the foot of the Big Horns, aiming for the mountain's north side and crossing Bad Water Creek at Lost Cabin. They journeyed on through Lost Cabin, then stayed awhile at the D Bar ranch.

Information taken from AGNES CHAMBERLIN written by Ester Johansson Murray, is being used with written permission.

Agnes wrote, "We stayed a day or two at Lost Cabin." She had nothing further to say about this famous place where John B. Okie built up a fabulous ranch and settlement with an elaborate home, and started the post office with himself as first postmaster (August 31, 1886). From Lost Cabin, they turned northerly up Bridger Creek, and like other travelers, finally encountered good water and better grass. It is likely they spotted their first mountain bluebirds in this habitat. Wolves, mountain lions, and big game were pretty well hunted out, but they could have seen bobcats, badgers, and a few coyotes.

As they traveled north Agnes wrote, " we stayed at D Ranch. It was just a ranch where a post office was located, and there were a grown son and daughter of the proprietor and also some hired men and a very gay divorced woman was cook to the outfit. The son played the guitar and they all sang 'coon songs' and the grass widow did some dance steps that brought down the house. We had a very pleasant stay there, and we both saw that the grass widow was making a play for the son of the family and the rest did not approve."

Further research revealed there was a post office called "Deranch", established January 19, 1893, and William Long served as first postmaster. The Deranch post office closed February 28, 1905. On an 1899 map of the area, the only ranch identified is DE Ranch on south-flowing Bridger Creek, a tributary of Bad Water Creek, north of Lost Cabin, the ranch the Chamberlins visited. According to John K. Rollinson in *Wyoming Cattle Trails*, Tom Turner started the D ranch in 1883, but sold out the next year to an "English Outfit".

Even at this higher elevation, summer heat brought out mosquitoes and horse flies and when the horses lathered up on the steep slopes, the sweat dried to salty white lines under the harness straps. White daisies and fading Indian paint brush colored some of the higher, wetter areas. After the Chamberlins topped the divide between Bridger Creek and Kirby Creek which flows into the Big Horn river, Agnes did not mention any ranches, but early settlers were Captain Cookesley and Brown who ran a horse ranch north of east Kirby Creek called "The Chimneys". Famous sheep queen of Wyoming, Ella Moore, ran the Kirby Creek Ranch by 1900, but apparently the Chamberlins did not encounter any of these people. Cody writer, Caroline Lockhart, researched material for her book *The Fighting Shepherdess* while staying in Ella Moore's sheep camp.

Agnes had nothing to say about the Thermopolis settlement. Although the Chamberlins stayed a month there, Agnes failed to mention the springs or the glowing white mineral deposits for which the town is famous. In 1897, the Shoshone Indians gave the land to the United States and the natural mineral springs were turned over to the state of Wyoming for a State Park. Three or four spas utilized the healing qualities of the hot mineral waters in 1900 and by 1902 the State administered the first public bath house.

Few people knew much about it. They read an issue of the *Cody Enterprise* and were favorably impressed so decided to travel over and have a look at the four-year-old town.

> Otto was platted in 1888, and named after Otto Franc, founder of the Pitchfork ranchup the Greybull river. It came to have two newspapers, and was the senior town in contention with Basin City for county seat. Basin won out and eventually the town of Otto declined. At this time, Probably The Otto Courier.

> From Otto they continued to Meeteetse, a picturesque town which had been established on Meeteetse Creek in 1881, but was moved to the Greybull river in 1893. This town took over the short-lived Otto Franc post office.

JO JEAN THOMAS DEHONY

On an 1899 map of the area the only ranch identified is DE Ranch on a south flowing tributary of Bad Water Creek, north of Lost Cabin, possibly this could be the ranch the Chamberlin's visited. The Chamberlin's traveled the old Bridger Trail north from Casper.

After fighting slippery side hills and gumbo roads up and over the Big Horns, They reached Thermopolis pretty well exhausted. Dewey's feet were raw from trotting over alkali flats. A kindly shopkeeper directed them to a vacant shack where they set up primitive housekeeping and Mark kept hoping for some dental work to come his way, but had few patients. Agnes lamented Mark had a good time gypsying over the country, hunting and fishing, but she had married for a home, security, respectability and felt like an outcast and ashamed of the way they lived.

During this time they asked the questions about the new settlement of Cody but as it was at the far end of the Big Horn Basin not much was known about it.

However they read the Cody Enterprise and were favorably impressed so decided to travel over and have a look. They went via Hyattville, then to Basin and Otto where they stayed a week. Mark set up his dental shop in the hotel and Agnes got work on the newspaper. It was before the spring runoff therefore little water flowed in the Greybull River, so the men could spear ling with pitchforks. Ling were, to the Chamberlin's, a new and unfishlike fish, unattractive but edible.

From Otto they continued to Meeteese stopping over in Mr. and Mrs. People's Hotel, a rugged shelter that served the traveler until 1902 when the Weller hotel opened. Dewey growled all night at mice scurrying behind the canvas covered walls. Tom Gillies, Forman for Richard Ashworth of the Z Bar T, invited the Chamberlin's to the ranch so Mark could work on the men's teeth. The locals informed the Chamberlin's that Ashworth was an English remittance man. A remittance person is one who lie s abroad or away from home on funds sent from home. Agnes, always perceptive of interpersonal relationships, noted Tom and the wife of one of the ranch hands were getting romantically involved.

When they started for Cody, Agnes and Mark followed their third pioneer trail, the Red Lodge—Meeteetse Trail, going past the post office at Wise (1894-1903) when John Corbett was first postmaster.). They descended the steep, mile long. Meeteetse Rim and turned north to Cody.

The first sign of civilization they saw was Mr. Beck's ice house on Beck Lake. Then they dropped off the south bench into Cody, (founded in May 1896) on August 26, 1900, and stayed in one of the two rental rooms of the Cody Hotel.

The Chamberlins soon found a small frame cabin to rent in the twelve hundred block on the north side of Sheridan Avenue, continuing to use the stove in the wagon for cooking. But soon bought a lot on the North side of Sheridan Avenue, exchanging dental work with Hud Darrah for lumber and construction of the two room cabin(Hud Darrah had an extensive sawmill on Carter Mountain.

Agnes and Dewey roamed the surrounding hill. Agnes carried a .22 rifle and sometimes successfully shot a rabbit or two for food. It is possible she knocked down a few sage hens. These sage grouse were very plentiful over most of Wyoming wherever sagebrush habitat existed. They quickly made progress, and got in the swing of what social life the pioneer town of Cody offered.

The Chamberlins received one of the ornate invitations for the November 18th opening and Agnes carefully saved it. Included in the invitation was the menu starting with the two choices of soup: consomme vermicelli or chicken giblet, followed by descriptions of relish, fish, entrees, roasts, salads, vegetables, dessert choices, and finally, coffee and cigars. One of Agnes' newspaper clippings described the women's gown Agnes' trunk had finally caught up with her and she wore figured dimity, (a fine, light weight cotton dress), trimmed with green velvet ribbons and cream lace.

Her piano arrived in 1902, also. Agnes probably enjoyed being called Mrs. Doctor Chamberlin, an added social bonus of the times.

Mark found an unused barber chair and set up his dental office in the cabin and soon Agnes started setting type for Colonel Peake, co-owner with Colonel Cody of the Cody Enterprise. With both working they quickly made progress, Mark exchanged dental work on Hud Darrah's teeth for lumber for a two room house, and they soon got in the swing of what social life in the pioneer town of Cody offered. Stone cutters from Thermopolis chipped away at gray sandstone in the construction of the Irma Hotel and its opening in November 1902 was the star studded event of the times and continued to be for decades afterwards. The women's gowns were described in the newspaper, Agnes' trunk had finally caught up with her and she wore figured dimity, a fine, light weight cotton dress, trimmed with green velvet ribbons and cream lace. Her piano arrived in 1902 also. Agnes probably enjoyed being called Mrs. Doctor Chamberlin, an added bonus of the times.

Col. Cody heavily invested in the area. In addition to the Irma hotel, named after his daughter and pictured below, his enterprises included the Cody Trading Company, a livery stable and the *Cody Enterprise*. In addition, near Meeteetse he purchased the Carter Ranch on the South Fork of the Stinking Water (now the South Fork of the Shoshone) which he named the T E.

Irma Letterhead, undated.
Property of Jo Jean DeHony

As indicated by the letterhead, Cody's brother-in-law, Louis Decker, was general manager of the hotel which opened in in 1902.

The Irma Hotel, shown here around 1920, opened in 1902.
It was named for the daughter of William F. "Buffalo Bill" Cody.
Courtesy of Wyoming Tales and Trails

Lower Left, Irma Hotel, 1908, photo by F. J. Hiscock
Courtesy of Wyoming Tales and Trails

The Irma was constructed by Cody in 1902 and was designed by famed Nebraska architect Alfred Wilderman Woods. Although intended as a luxury hotel, some guests were less than impressed. In 1916, Horace M. Albright (1890-1987) escorted National Park System Director Stephen Tyng Mather (1867-1930) on a tour to Yellowstone. On the first night of the tour, the Mather party stayed at the Irma. In his *Creating the National Park Service: the Missing Years*, Horace M. Albright and Marian Albright Schenck, University of Oklahoma Press, Norman, 1999, Albright gave an account of the stay. The dinner was a disaster, with bad food and terrible service. Albright at the request of Director Mather checked the kitchen. "It was about the dirtiest, most unsanitary place I had ever seen." According to Albright,

The rest of the evening turned out to be equally bad. First of all, Mrs. Mather insisted on sitting up all night in the lobby after she discovered "things crawling in the bed." Mather ordered a pillow and blankets for her, saw to her comfort, and then disappeared back to the lice, bedbugs, or whatever.

He didn't last long there because when he opened the door to his room he found two men asleep in his bed. Downstairs at the desk he demanded another room. "there is no other room," said the clerk. "You'll just have to make your bedfellows move over." He soon saw a strange **man crawling into his bed. As he lay awake listening to the snores of his bedmate, he became aware of the "various bugs that had missed Mrs. Mather," and thus moved to the floor.**

However before the opening of the Irma, Agnes had two memorable adventures which will be mentioned herewith. The first occurred in the spring of 1902 and reveals great deal about Agnes' Courage and compassion. At this time her and Mark were living compatibly and she had quit setting type and gotten her stride with her own business interests. In her memoirs she tells that a cousin of Mark's, Walter Pickens and his wife Ella arrived in Cody looking for work. The Chamberlins found work for them on Otto Franc's Pitchfork ranch up the Greybull River south of Meeteese. That winter Ella wrote Agnes that she was expecting a baby and asked Agnes if she could come over for a few days and help her sew to buy baby clothes nor purchase a layette for a new born. In those days it was neither common practice to buy baby clothes nor to purchase a layette for a newborn. Later towards spring, they considered it safe for Agnes to set forth.

Agnes stated that mark hitched up the team for her very early one morning and she set out alone for the Pitchfork.

Agnes had been over the route when they came from Thermopolis via Meeteese to Cody. Apparently the weather cooperated and all went well on the trip. When she arrived at the ranch there were so many men to cook for that both Walter and Ella worked in the kitchen and it impressed her that Walter made lovely bread. Agnes and Ella sewed for a week and the day Agnes decided to return home it turned windy and cold with intermittent snow. Walter heated "boulders" to put in the wagon for her feet and she set forth.

She apparently traveled the old Meeteese trail to the Wise post office. From there she decided to keep following the old trail rather than going eastward to a newer road. As she drove along she met a horseback rider but she chose not to speak to him. Courtesy demanded she speak first or he could not engage her in conversation. As the horses plodded along, the road became more and more difficult, finally impassable from drifted snow and she had to turn around and retrace he route to the other road. She again encountered the rider. This time she spoke to him and he rebuked her for not speaking the first time so he could have advised her about road conditions, saving her much time and trouble. In her memoirs she wrote she took his rebuke as kindly and well deserved. She explained she was like her father, not wanting to ask advice and said "father always failed in whatever he attempted".

During her day traveling she faced snow squalls between long stretches of brilliant sun reflecting off the snow. She arrived home with a bad case of "snow burn", resulting in swollen face and burned skin that eventually peeled off. She did not mention any snow blindness. The conditions she encountered sound like capricious March weather. The Cody Enterprise for May 29, 1902, had a news item stating the baby of Mr. and Mrs. Walter Pickens had been very ill and Dr. Brandbury and Dr. Gillam had treated the child. Agnes wrote the

Pickens' returned to Nebraska and she didn't see them again for twenty years. She probably would have mentioned if the baby died.

1902 TRIP TO YELLOWSTONE

The fall of 1902, Mark, Agnes, and Dewey took their first trip through Yellowstone Park. While planning the trip they had requested a copy of Park regulations. Among Agnes' memorabilia is *Rules and Regulations of the Yellowstone National Park*, Dated February 7, 1902. Under "Instructions to Persons Traveling through the Park" we find advice to carefully control camp fires. Second, is advice for setting up camp sites: care must be taken when hanging blankets as hammocks. Any items that might frighten the teams must not be used. Bicycle riders must take care not to frighten the horses. When fishing, release fish under six inches. Dogs must not run free. Care must be taken not to overgraze when pasturing the horses, and lastly, no carving of names anywhere. This was signed by : Jno. Pitcher, Major, 6th Cavalry, USA. Acting Superintendent of Yellowstone National Park. From 1889 to 1916 Army officers were detailed as acting superintendents of the park, so when the Chamberlins traveled through it, the Army patrolled and controlled.

The itinerary for this trip included the Sunlight Basin and Cooke City and return by way of Dubois and Meeteetse. Mark planned it as a hunting trip rather than a sightseeing trip.

Cody Road, Winter, approx. 1910.
Courtesy of Wyoming Tales and Trails

JO JEAN THOMAS DEHONY

The "Corkscrew," Sylvan Pass, Cody Road
Courtesy of Wyoming Tales and Trails

The "Loop" or "Corkscrew" was originally constructed in 1903 and was replaced in 1919 by the structure in the next three photos.

The "Corkscrew," Sylvan Pass, Cody Road, photo by F. J. Hiscock
Courtesy of Wyoming Tales and Trails

In 1929, the road was relocated to the side of the canyon and thus for years the structure was not visible from the road.

Mark wanted to be in the hunting area south of Yellowstone when the moose season opened, so they started out on their four week trip traveling via Sunlight and Clarks Fork. Until 1903, when the Sylvan Pass road via the new

East Entrance to Yellowstone was opened, the Clarks Fork route was provided the closest wagon road for visiting Yellowstone Par from Cody.

As early as 1885, a wagon road to Cooke City over Dead Indian from Red Lodge area had been financed and constructed by Billings Men. The road had not been well-maintained after being built.

They faced a dangerously steep descent down the west side of Dead Indian Hill. Mark did not rough lock his rear wheels, but cut down a very large pine tree and tied it to the back of the wagon. The crushed needles of dragging the tree would have filled the air with the smell of pitch and raised a cloud of dust. At this higher altitude, black and grey Clark's nutcrackers flew through the timber, cawing to each other, breaking the mountain silence.

He unhitched the team and tied them to the rear of the wagon to help hold it back, and everyone walked to the bottom where they relaxed and ate lunch at Dead Indian Creek. They discarded the tree which joined the others that littered the bottom of the hill. The next adventure occurred at Sunlight Creek Where the road had washed out. Mark again tied a rope to the back of the wagon and helped restrain its progress while Agnes, on the upper side of the hill, walked and drove the team. They got across safely, but she said dropping off the many rocky "reefs" farther along the route proved difficult.

To the west of Cody, the South and North Forks of the Stinking Water combine. In 1902 the Legislature renamed the River as the Shoshone.

Bridge over Shoshone River, 1911
Courtesy of Wyoming Tales and Trails

JO JEAN THOMAS DEHONY

The river had been discovered and named in 1807-08 trapping expeditions on behalf of Manuel de Lisa by John Colter. The river took its name of Stinking Water from the sulphurous springs near Cody.

From Ester Johansson Murray

The next adventure occurred at Sunlight Creek where the road had washed out.

Mark again tied a rope to the back of the wagon and helped restrain its progress while Agnes, on the upper side of the hill, walked and drove the team. They got across safely, but she said dropping off the many rocky reefs farther along the route proved difficult.

There is only one prominent reef evident in the mountain on the south side of the valley from Sunlight Creek all the way to the west end of the Clarks Fork drainage near Pilot Creek. Agnes probably referred to the granite outcroppings along the primitive wagon trail. Sparks flew out from the horse shoes and tire rims striking the granite strata.

John R. Painter, pioneer rancher and miner had settled up Sunlight Creek and started the first post office in the area, December 1902, which ran until October 1950.

The excellent fishing in the deep green pools of the Clarks Fork river, near their crossing, provided a delicious meal. Before they reached Cooke City they passed the empty wooden buildings of the defunct Republic Smelter that had been started with high hopes of great riches being mined, but failure to get a railroad caused the venture to collapse and other mineral discoveries never revived the boom. The Republic Smelter was built in 1883 and began operating in 1884 for a short time. Mining revived in 1904, under New World Smelting Company, but failed in1908.

> On the third day, they reached Cooke City, and Agnes worried that the town of Cody might experience a similar boom and bust.

The Chamberlins' hit the trail to Lamar valley and to Mammoth, over to West Thumb and south to Moran as speedily as possible because Mark wanted to reach the hunting area. Agnes did not comment on the geysers or scenery on this trip.

At Moran, Mark rented two more horses so they had two riding horses and two pack horses for their hunt. They headed for Bridger Lake.

Written by Agnes Chamberlin

The excellent fishing at their Clarks Fork River crossing provided a delicious meal. Then the third day they reached Cooke City and Agnes worried that the town of Cody might experience a similar boom and bust.

On to the Lamar Valley and to Mammoth, over the West thumb and South to Moran went speedily as Mark wanted to reach the hunting area. At Moran Mark rented two more horses so they had two riding horses and two pack horses for their hunt. They headed for Bridger Lake. Always an avid seamstress, Agnes, before the trip made herself what she called a little suit of pants and jacket for mountain climbing, but she also wore when on the horseback riding stint of their trip. There are photographs of Agnes on horseback at other times, wearing the popular long, divided skirt that had a panel that buttoned down the side to become a conventional skirt when not riding. When not riding she wore the long, heavy skirt and blouse appropriate for the times. What Agnes remembered vividly about this part of the trip was the extremely cold September nights causing them to sleep cold. Dewey usually slept at their feet but one particularly cold night he kept inching his way up between them and almost crowded them out of bed.

Despite climbing up and down every mountain side they failed to find any game, except for one elk near Towgotee Pass which Dewey chased away and ruined their chance. Mark became so angry with the dog that when they got back to the ranger station Mark begged the ranger to shoot Dewey. The ranger gave Mark a lecture about man's best friend, Mark repented and Dewey happily followed them back to Cody. Dewey hated being restrained and leashed while they traveled through Yellowstone.

From Moran they followed the same route on the way to Dubois Mark shot and wounded a wolf. He tracked it and killed it but Agnes lamented he got blood all over his clean corduroy shirt. Mark believed the stock association would pay him $20 bounty. He hung the wolf on the back of the wagon so he could skin it when they camped for the night. He learned the stock association no longer paid a bounty but he decided to take the hide back to Cody.

> They were invited to take a meal with the famous Dubois storekeeper family, the Wetly's, and their affluence and fine style of living greatly impressed Agnes. Like Ashworth on the Greybull River, the Wetly's had a large supply of books and magazines.

> Then on down the Wind River until they hit the Red Lodge-Meeteese-Rawlins stage route over the Owl Creek Mountains. After his arduous hunting and

camping chores they agreed Mark should take a nap in the back of the wagon and Agnes would drive the team. She held the reins and dreamily let the team follow the road without much supervision, but this resulted in a serious accident to the wagon. The horses hit a gully too hard and broke the wagon reach, a wagon cannot travel with a broken reach, which is the stout pole or 2x4 connecting the front and back axles on the underside of the wagon. To repair a broken reach another hole must be drilled or it could be temporarily repaired with bailing wire. Mark wired it together and it held until going down off the Owl Creek Mountains when it broke again. This time the only solution was to bore another hole in the reach in order to put the pin through to hold the running gears of the wagon together. With no tool for boring the hole the only solution would be to burn a hole in the hardwood pole. They unhitched the team, took no time to prepare supper but built a fire so Mark could heat the king pin to red hot and pound it repeatedly on the reach, slowly burning a hole. Agnes kept gathering sage brush for the fire and by ten o'clock that night the hole was ready, the task completed, and the exhausted pair collapsed in bed.

Getting home after four weeks of primitive travel seemed pretty good. Mark had the pelt of a wolf, but this is what Agnes thought of their 1902 hunting-camping trip, "We brought back with us nothing but our memories of one of the hardest, most agonizing experiences, I have ever had in my life".

YELLOWSTONE TRIP 1903

Fortunately, by the summer of 1903 Agnes' mood had changed and they planned another trip to Yellowstone Park. Her sister Bertha arrived for a visit and naturally wanted to tour the Park. Besides Agnes, Mark and Bertha they invited Mrs. India Hess, called "Hessie", stenographer for the Cody Trading Company, to round our the party. Sadly Dewey was missing. This time they traveled in style because they hired a light wagon and a good team.

By Ester Johansson Murray

Dewey had figured in all they did, but after a couple years in Cody, he was poisoned. This must have been disturbing to everyone because in the records of the city council meeting for March 9, 1904, George T. Beck, prominent founder of Cody, petitioned the council to make it a crime and misdemeanor to poison dogs. Agnes wrote that when Dewey passed away, they both grieved. Agnes said,

"I put his body in a gunny sack and carried him by horseback down by the river and buried him."

It's possible that for this trip, they had considered going with some local outfitter because Agnes saved a four-page brochure printed on yellow paper, "Borron Brothers—Marquette, Wyo." in which they describe their camping trips. This would be Lee and Bill Borron. Later, both Lee and Bill worked for Dwight Hollister on the North Fork, and for many years Bill worked at Holm Lodge for Billy Howell and Miss Shawver.

Pahaska Teepee, undated
Courtesy of Wyoming Tales and Trails

In 1901 Col. Cody selected the site for the Pahaska Teepee 1 1/2 miles from the entrance to Yellowstone Park. The hotel was located at the confluence of the North Fork of the Shoshone and Middle Creek. Pahaska was an Indian name for Cody.

Even though Yellowstone National Park is primarily in Wyoming, prior to 1899 the only practical access to the Park was through Montana. Consideration of the construction of a wagon road from Wyoming into the Park dates back as far as 1881 when Territorial Governor John W. Hoyt visited the Park with the view of locating a route for a road into the Park without the necessity of traveling into Idaho and Montana. Government tends to move slowly and it was not until 1899, that a wagon road was constructed from Fort Washakie to Yellowstone over Togwotee Pass.

Governor Hoyt in his annual report discussed a route along the North Fork of the Stinking Water earlier explored by Capt. William A. Jones in 1873. Governor Hoyt noted the advantages and disadvantages of the route:

Cody Road, 1907, photo by F. J. Hiscock
Courtesy of Wyoming Tales and Trails

Construction of the road along the Stinking Water, however, did not occur until 1903. As indicated in the photo, the road was little more than a trail. The Pahaska was opened for business in 1904, although not completed until 1905. Rates at the hotel were $3.00 a day or $15.00 a week. Amenities included baths and a long distance telephone.

On his 1916 inspection tour Park Service Director Mather was no more impressed with the Pahaska that he was with the Irma. Albright later wrote:

Earlier in the day, Mather wishing to inspect the Shoshone Dam, had ordered his chauffeur to break off a padlock on the gate which impeded

Director Mather's inspection and had ordered a dam attendant to demolish unsightly buildings.

Hunting Party led by Col. Cody, 1907
Courtesy of Wyoming Tales and Trails

Cody's autumn hunting parties were not without risk. *The New York Tribune*, October 30, 1906, reported that one of his parties with British army officers and several Austrians were lost in an October blizzard. They were not really lost, but were delayed by several days by the snow.

East Entrance to Park at Sylvan Pass, 1909.
Courtesy of Wyoming Tales and Trails

JO JEAN THOMAS DEHONY

Early visitors to the Park were required to either leave their side arms at the entrance or have them sealed.

They made the trip in ten days, considered pretty fast for a Park tour. Also, they could travel on a brand new road directly up the North Fork over Sylvan Pass into the Park. They saw the sights and did a lot of fishing. Like most early travelers, Agnes commented on the wormy fish from Yellowstone Lake. Agnes wrote the fish had "dark spots with coiled parasitic worms inside". Many travelers wrote about these fish such as early explorer Lt. Jones of the 1873 Expedition through Yellowstone. Also Caroline Lockhart in her novel The Dude Wrangler (1921) built an episode of a camp cook who crispy fried a large, wormy trout and in revenge, fed it to a dudine whom he hated.

The following was taken from the Agnes Chamberlin book written by Ester Johansson Murray

MEMORABILIA

In a shallow, woven basket with a six inch diameter, Agnes kept a few, very old calling cards: "Miss Agnes Brown"; "Mrs. Mark Chamberlin"; "Mark Chamberlin, Dentist, Woodward, Okla. One door west of Post Office". There was a dance program, "1896, New Year Eve Dance, Woodward, Okla." A hand-scripted calling card with the name "J. T. Vandervoort—W. C. College, 1898" is not identified. Was he one of her lost loves she met at Woodward Commercial College?

Other small, white calling cards reveal the socialites of early Cody: a 1-1/2" by 3" card with the name of Mrs. J. H. Peake, (engraved in script); Mrs. George Thornton Beck and Miss Thompson left engraved cards. Mrs. L. L. Newton, Miss Nelle Traugh, and Miss Claunch left small hand written cards. A 2 3/4" by 3 " envelope addressed to Mrs. Dr. Chamberlin, Cody, contained the following card: Mrs. F. C. Barnett and Mrs. W. B. Nuchols—March 18th " 2:30 to 5" o'clock—China Shower for Miss Kissick.

Items in Agnes' little woven basket give a glimpse into the social life going on in the raw, new settlement of Cody, with its unpaved streets, no sidewalks, no trees or grass, but plenty of wind. Another invitation mailed to Mrs. Chamberlin, City, contained the card "Mrs. A. R. Williams with Mrs. Wm. Loewer—Monday March 21st at 2 to 5:30-Granit (sic) Shower for Miss Kissick." The arrival of C.B. & Q. R.R. (Chicago, Burlington and Quincy Railroad) in November 1901, brought Burlington railroad agent, W.J. Kissick and wife to Cody. They had seven daughters; it is unknown how many daughters came to Cody with them. Frank Williams married Clara Kissick.

An envelope with its pink one-cent stamp, and addressed to Mrs. M. Chamberlin, Cody, Wy, contained the following formal note: "It will afford me much pleasure to accept your kind invitation as guest of honor Thursday, July tenth. Please accept my sincere thanks for the compliment bestowed." Signed, "Very cordially yours, Claire Belle Green" Across the lower corner of the page is written "Cody, July ninth /02".

Most invitations were eagerly accepted, but occasionally a rejection appeared such as the message on a folded paper in an envelope and delivered to "Mrs. M. Chamberlin, City". The message stated: "Miss Link regrets that, due to school duties, she cannot accept Mrs. Chamberlin's 'at home' this afternoon. Oct. 26 1903". These notes seem ostentatious, but were quite proper for the times; phone service had come to Cody in 1903, (Rocky Mountain Bell Telephone had the franchise), but very few had telephones. An envelope addressed to Mrs. Chamberlin had the following note inside: "Mrs. Atherton Clark and Mrs. L. L. Newton are pleased to accept the kind invitation of Mrs. Chamberlain (sic) for Monday afternoon, October twenty six, nineteen naught three."

And the Chamberlins received an invitation for the Dedication of M E Church, Cody, Wyoming July 20, 1902, Rev. E. E. Tarbil!.

One invitation to Dr. M. Chamberlin did not include his wife. It stated "You are respectfully invited to attend the opening of my new residence at Cody, Wyo.

November 1st, 1902. (Signed) Miss Etta Feeley". Etta Feeley (aka Alice Leach, 1870-1960) came to Cody from Billings, Montana, via Red Lodge, Montana. An early photo shows a good looking woman with white karakul lamb fur jacket and grandly plumed hat.

On December 16, 1901, the Cody Town Council granted her a liquor license. She built a large, two-story, $4,000.00 white house on the east end of Bleistein Avenue where she ran her brothel. Her business proved profitable and by 1903, she invested $600.00 in improvements. Also, according to Cody Town Council minutes, fines against Etta Feeley (and later other madams and their businesses) helped keep the town's finances solvent.

A newspaper article for December 1900, said, "This blooming town has become fairly ablaze here of late with social functions". The word "booming" might have been just as accurate as "blooming". There were many marriages, showers, and card parties, cribbage, and progressive whist (a card game) mentioned in the social column of the paper. Of course, in a few years this formality fell away.

People were pre-occupied with their social lives, and with all that was going on, Agnes got so busy that after her 1903 trip to Yellowstone she didn't get back for eighteen years. In 1921 she arranged a six-day trip to the park. She drove her Oldsmobile and her guests were Mrs. Hanson, Mrs. Poole (Frank Blackburn's sister), and Mabel Watson, her faithful assistant for many years. Mabel Watson worked for the Dr. Bennett family in Meeteetse for seven years and when the Bennetts moved to Cody and Dr. Bennett's practice and finances failed, she began working for Mrs. Chamberlin in 1910, and stayed with her. When Mabel's health failed she was cared for by Agnes, and Mabel (1885-1939) was buried in the Chamberlin cemetery plot, as was Robert A. Blair, (1860-1942) long time handyman at the Hotel.

Information from notes found in Hotel

Agnes got so busy she didn't get back to Yellowstone for eighteen years. In 1921 she arranged a six day trip, she drove her Oldsmobile and her guests were a Mrs. Hanson, Mrs. Poole (Frank Blackburn's sister); and Mabel Watson, Her faithful assistant for many years.

The long progression in upgrading their dwelling from the frame house they built on the large property they bought between Sheridan and Rumsey Avenues, about a sixth of a town block. The big project of the 1917 Hotel, was difficult to follow.

Inserted at this point is information given by Jo Jean DeHony of what was changed after she purchased the Hotel.

The Pawnee Hotel gives the appearance of one large unit, but inside there have been alterations and additions too numerous to untangle.

In 1939 Agnes sold her hotel to Hattie and George Edwards; in 1941 they changed the name to Pawnee and in 1974 Jo Jean DeHony bought it and began remodeling and upgrading.

THE FOLLOWING INFORMATION WAS RELATED BY JO JEAN DEHONY

In February of 2003, present owner, Jo Jean cheerfully provided a guided tour of the upstairs and downstairs, pointing out where tasteful wallpaper covers old brick partitions. In the eighteen original rooms, somewhat altered from the 1917 construction, are original windows, corner sinks, and radiators. The tiny closets have been enlarged and many bathrooms added, some bathrooms have the large, original tubs. Agnes had one public bathroom on the second floor, this is now a communal bathroom serving a couple bedrooms that does not have private baths. The communal bathroom was also used my many rooms that had only tubs and the guest wanted a shower.

The original stairway to the second floor is still in use. In the lower hallway are the original three pronged coat hooks, also the original looped fire hose is attached to a water faucet. The original fifty feet of two inch wide hose is still neatly folded in a rack that could be swung outward from the wall.

In the present office is the original red brick fireplace with a wide four foot opening, so well constructed it still draws nicely according to the present owner. A small telephone exchange with twenty connections is still kept as a memento.

Whether Agnes had that installed is not known. Still in use in the front vestibule are four very nice doors, each with twelve panels of beveled glass.

There was a laundry shoot from the second floor to the basement laundry room. In the basement are two sections separated by a firewall, probably from two different constructions. The square, wooden laundry shoot from the second floor with its basement door is closed to the location of original laundry facilities.

On the north basement side is the original very primitive would automatically open the water valve to the long, narrow vertical water tank, activating the flushing process.

Off the south side the hotel, was a well traveled alley where in the early 1900's was the coal chute. The coal would be unloaded into a basement room and stockpiled in a large separate coal room. The original furnace was east of the coal room, handy to its door making it easy to shovel he coal from the coal room into the furnace.

Agnes ended up with 18 rooms. Jo Jean ended with twenty two rooms to rent, along with a couple of rooms for storage, and the large living quarters, occupied by Jo Jean and her mother Erma.

From the upper hallway there was access to an attic where old memorabilia were stored, dance cards, original menu for the opening of the Irma, small flags in bundles, old cuff buttons, and also included glass photo plates which Jo Jean had developed. The pictures were of Indians, on horses, and appeared to be on the lot north of the hotel? At this date they were unidentified as to tribe.

In the 1917 kitchen the builders installed a large cement slab on which Agnes' new double oven Majestic cook stove stood and behind the stove, tin sheeting on the wall gave fire protection. Her large dining room was on the west side of the kitchen, and led into the hallway that took you down the long hallway passed down-stair rooms and west into the front Lobby.

We will now continue with more of the information gathered from articles in the Cody Enterprise.

EARLY HOTELS

Earlier in this story, was discussion of the Hotel Chamberlin, along with a number of early hotels and rooming houses H. K. Barbee rented beds and/ or a space to throw down a bedroll in a frame cabin and a tent. This was on the corner of 13th Street and Sheridan Avenue where the first Cody Trading Company stood. His wife, Mrs. Barbee was the first white woman in Cody.

INFORMATION FROM
ESTER JOHANSSON MURRAY

Soon Badland Dave McFall built the Hart Mountain Hotel 1897-98; R. C. Hargraves bought Badland Dave McFall's ranch on Cottonwood Creek north of Cody, and Dave and his fashionable wife built the Hart Mountain Inn, 1897-98.

(Mrs. Aurilla Horr married David F. McFall at his ranch on Cottonwood, on the evening of March 24, 1898-second marriage that day for Justice Charles Hayden). One source on file at the Park County Archives says the Inn was the first two-story building in Cody—or was the Schwoob house on Alger avenue the first two-story house? Hillis Jordan and wife, May Edick Jordan, bought the Hart Mountain Inn from the McFall family around 1912, and ran it unti11928. Much later, its last owner, colorful Kate Buckingham, ran it and lived there until it closed in the 1990's. In 2004, the enlarged, restored and enhanced building now owned by Simeon Stoddard, became Hart Mountain Suites on the corner of 13th and Beck.

The Cody Hotel is listed on main street by 1896, (north side of 1300 block of Sheridan Avenue). In 1896, the first school classes were conducted in the Cody Hotel with first teacher Vida Weborg, and she organized the town's first Christmas celebration in the school. In September of 1900, there is mention in the Cody paper of Gus Holms, early contractor, building a Ketchum Hotel which seems to have been short lived, or perhaps had a change of name? If the old news reports are accurate, it states that "Coldwater Bill" sold the Cody Hotel to Mrs. Turnbull who sold it Mr. Shurtleff, and was operated by O. D. Marx. In 1900, Marx also ran a saloon in the hotel which at that time consisted of two rental rooms, and when the tired Chamberlins arrived in Cody, they stayed in one of them. Later, more rooms were added. J. B. "Ben" Primm owned the Cody Hotel and saloon in 1903, (Ben kept pet black bear cubs that ran freely on the streets of Cody), and by 1908 Katie Primm ran it, and later Lonnie Prante, and it stayed in business until 1932. Before the Cody Presbyterians built their church, they were hard pressed to find locations for suppers and other money raising events. According to their minutes a fund raiser was held September 22, 1909. "Sister Goodman reported that arrangements had been made to hold our supper in the old Ben Primm Saloon. The name to be painted over by Mr. Schwoob Mrs. Goodman was Buffalo Bill's sister and Jakie Schwoob was an early entrepreneur and manager of Cody Trading Company.

Charles DeMaris (1827-1914) trailed cattle from Lemhi Valley, Idaho, via Montana to the Trail Creek area on the Stinking Water River of Wyoming in April of 1886. He was in poor health and was accompanied by a doctor. *(Buffalo Bill's Town in the Rockies* places the date in 1883). He had heard of the medicinal springs east of the canyon between Cedar and Rattlesnake Mountains because the healing waters of the mineral springs had long been used by native Americans. Here he took up homestead land and regained his health in the springs which came to carry the white man's name: DeMaris Needlebath Springs. The first wedding in Cody was Charles DeMaris and Nellie Fitzgerald, March 24, 1898, at the home of Nellie's aunt, Mrs. Jerry Ryan.

DeMaris Springs, approx. 1910
Courtesy of Wyoming Tales and Trails

The small shed depicted in the image was in place at least by 1897 and was heated in the winter by a stove. The water from the springs were bottled for their medicinal value by William Yager who later founded the Cody Bottling Works. Other settlers came: Pat O'Hara after whom the creek is named; George Marquette who came in 1881; Charles L. Green; and Charles A. Davis.

JO JEAN THOMAS DEHONY

Taken from Agnes Chamberlin
written by Ester Johansson Murray

The first hostelry at the DeMaris Springs consisted of a low, one-story log cabin called the "Undercliff Hotel", run by Mrs. M. P. Edick. (In 1901, she married John Dyer, a prominent cowboy with a long rope (i.e. a cattle rustler). They soon moved to Musselshell, Montana. The hotel that DeMaris built at his Springs in 1902, at a cost of $5,000.00, served more as a spa for individuals recuperating and for those bathing in the medicinal waters, or "taking the cure". In the small space between the north cliff and the river bank, and east of the main springs, he built his large, two-story frame building graced by a long porch on the south side overlooking the green water, yellow sulfur deposits and red cliffs. Very noticeable from the Springs all the way to Cody, emanated the heavy "rotten egg" smell of sulfur which met with various reactions from tolerance to extreme dislike. At this time the Springs were reached from the old North Fork road that crossed the river at the Depot bridge and traveled west on the north side of the river. In 1916, Mrs. Chase was proprietor and ran this hotel located deep in the canyon. The popular swimming pool was used continuously over the years, but the hotel fell into disuse. After World War II, Nick and Faye Knight remodeled the hotel into a nightclub and named it the Bronze Boot after the bronzed boot of Nick's cowboy pal, Fritz Truan, who died at Iwo Jima. It opened in April of 1946, and later Jimmy and Hilda Knight Ratliff took over the operation. A bridge was built near the Bronze Boot connecting with the North Fork highway on the south side of the river. This bridge washed out one time and was replaced in 1965. The old DeMaris Hotel/Bronze Boot burned to the ground April **11**, 1961, two months after Hilda had opened a newly built Bronze Boot on the south bench above the springs, between the highway and the canyon.

In 1902, Colonel William F. Cody built the Irma Hotel and named it after his daughter, Irma Cody Garlow. It was the heart of downtown Cody, and all four buildings facing the intersection had diagonal entrances and were built of the same grey sandstone.

The Irma has a fireplace of stones from many countries and a hand-carved cherry wood bar brought from Europe by the Colonel. Much of the hotel is original and much has been altered and enlarged. It is an historical treasure.

Other hotels have come and gone, and a notable few will be mentioned. In Cody, Dr. Ainsworth bought the Lane-Bradbury hospital (north west corner of 12th and Bleistein) and it eventually evolved into the Ainsworth Inn which ran for awhile. The Ross Hotel, under a different early name, was started by a Mrs. Austin from Thermopolis, sister of Fred Gail, an early Cody builder. It stood on the south side in the 1400 block of Sheridan Avenue and she sold to Zachery and Mary Ross, probably around 1915. It provided living quarters for the Rosses and three rooms and bath for rent on the second floor. They ran it as a residential hotel until 1928. Their daughter, Mrs. Grace Worst, kept the name Ross Hotel and ran it until 1951. This stucco-on-wood frame building was demolished in 1978. In 2003, Betty Jean Worst Rogers remembered her grandfather Ross with long grey beard, sitting in the lobby with his caged canaries, his gold fish, and a green parrot that would chase Betty Jean. Besides the indoor aquarium, the Rosses were the first in Cody to have an outdoor fish pond with large goldfish.

By far the largest hotel came to be built by the C. B. & Q.R.R. at the depot across the river. It carried the name, Cody Inn, but everyone called it the Burlington Inn. It started out small. In 1917 because of heavy railroad tourist travel there was a definite need for a large hotel. The C.B. & Q. R. R endeavored to get the town of Cody to build such accommodations but the town couldn't swing it, so in 1921 the railroad decided to build and in the spring of 1922 they began seeking bids for a large hotel just west of their depot and wool loading building. In 1924 they added twenty-five more rooms, giving them a total of ninety rooms, and their large dining room could accommodate at least four hundred guests. This mainly filled the need for summer tourists arriving by train, but the dining room and dance area remained open year around toward the end of its existence.

After World War II, it became a white elephant to the Burlington Railroad. Cowgill Agency bought it and began dismantling it in August of 1957. Husky Oil bought some of the buildings and moved them to the refinery for offices and some sections were moved east of the Holiday Inn for office space.

WRITTEN BY AGNES CHAMBERLIN

Colonel Cody Built the Irma Hotel 1902; in 1896 there was a Cody Hotel and by 1900 Mr. Marx ran the Cody Hotel, consisting of two rental rooms, on the north side 1300 block of Sheridan Avenue. When the tired Chamberlin' first arrived in Cody, they stayed in one of them. Later more rooms were added. J. B. "Ben" Primm owned the Cody Hotel and Saloon in 1903, (Ben kept pet black bear cubs that ran freely on the streets of Cody this was previously mentioned in connection with Dr Chamberlin enjoying the wild animals, while Agnes enjoyed the domestic animals), and by 1908 Kati Primm ran it and it stayed in business until 1932. Dr. Ainsworth bought the old Lane-Bradbury hospital (north west corner of 13th and Bleistein) and it eventually evolved into the Ainsworth Inn which ran for awhile.

The Ross Hotel, under an early name, was started by a Mrs. Mrs Austin Mrs. Austin sold to Zachary and Mary Ross probably around 1915. It provided living quarters for the Ross' with three rooms and bath for rent on the second floor. They ran it until 1928, then their daughter, Mrs. Grace Worst who kept the name "Ross Hotel".

This stucco on wood frame building was demolished in 1978. In 2003, Betty Jean Worst Rogers remembered her grandparent's birds and gold fish in the lobby on the main floor of the Ross Hotel.

When the buildings were brought into Cody from Wiley Town in Oregon Basin, the one placed on the north—west corner of Sheridan and 10th street in 1923 became the Trumble Inn and later changed to Green Gables and by 2003 is called Maxwell's. By far the largest hotel came to be built by the C.B. and Q Rail Road at the depot across the river and carried the name "Cody Inn", but everyone called it the Burlington Inn.

Burlington Depot and Inn, approx. 1927
Courtesy of Wyoming Tales and Trails

As a result of Cody's interest in the area, the Burlington System extended a spur to Cody in 1901. Even after the arrival of the railroad, the 130 mile ride from Toluca, Montana, was still an all day trip. Toluca, itself, was described by big game hunter A. H. Cordier as consisting of a "depot, a section house two Cody hotel signs and a large prairie dog population." Dr. Cordier noted that the length of the journey included stops the "engineer and fireman made when they went to shoot prairie chickens along the right of way." Cody was, according to Dr. Cordier, more animated because of the ranchmen, miners and cowboys than its size would otherwise indicate.

Col. Cody envisioned tourists arriving in Cody by train and then traveling by stage to Yellowstone up a road following the Shoshone River and staying in the Pahaska Tepee and Wapiti Inn. On the return, he envisioned the tourists staying in the Irma.

In 1917 because of heavy railroad tourist travel there was a definite need for a large hotel. The C.B.&Q Rail Road endeavored to get the town of Cody to build such accommodations but the town couldn't swing it, so in 1921 they decided to build, and in the spring of 1922 the railroad began seeking bids for a large hotel just west of their depot and wool loading building. In 1924 they added twenty five more rooms, giving them a total of ninety rooms. Their large dining room could accommodate at least four hundred guests. This mainly filled the need for summer tourists arriving by train. The dining room and dance area remained open year around toward the end of their existence.

After World War II it became a white elephant to the Burlington Railroad. Cowgill Agency bought it and began dismantling it in August of 1957. Husky Oil bought some of the buildings and moved them to the refinery for offices and some sections were moved to east of the Holiday Inn for office space

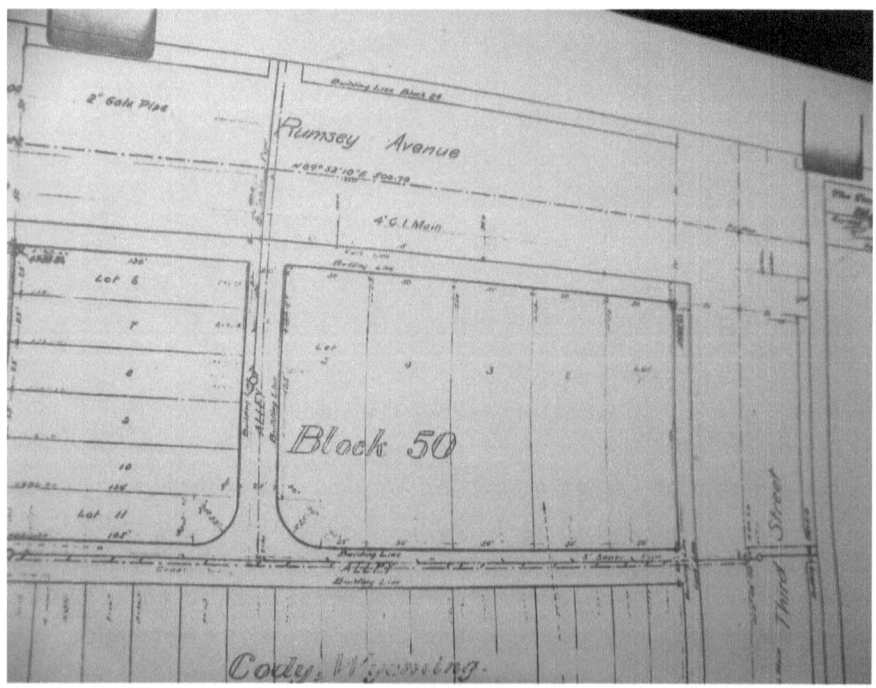

Park County Archives

BY ESTER JOHANSSON MURRAY

An article in the *Cody Enterprise* for September 6, 1900, states the Chamberlins bought a lot on Sheridan Avenue, and planned to build "a well built barn on rear of the lot." Before the Hotel Chamberlin, Agnes ran her boarding house. Legal documents researched by Jo Jean DeHony, show the Chamberlins bought Lot 11 of Block 50, from the Lincoln Land Company on February 10, 1903, and on May 27, 1904, they bought Lot 10, of Block 50. George T. Beck was agent for Lincoln Land Company. The Chamberlin' moved off Sheridan Avenue, (Main Street), around the corner to 12th Street in the spring of 1904, (they moved their barn across the alley) when Hud Darrah, in exchange for more dental work, plus monetary payment, furnished the lumber and built their two-story frame house which became the core of the complex on Lot 11 of Block 50. Darrah built it with a pitched roof behind a false front, facing 12th Street (at that time known as 2nd St.) and the main road from the Irma Hotel to the Depot.

Jo Jean DeHony collection

Two views of the Chamberlin Hotel, re-produced from photographs in Mrs. Chamberlin's scrapbook, now in the pos-session of Margaret Hamlin. In the photograph on the left, the original frame building is visible with Doc Chamberlin's

From the *Wyoming Industrial Journal* for 1906, published in Laramie, a photo shows the two-story, white frame boarding house. Dr.

Chamberlin's office is mentioned and he conducted his dental business in the front room.

Agnes' collected clippings in Park County Archives include a newspaper article for September 23, 1909, stating Dr. Chamberlin planned to build a 20 by 20 foot, brick office building. A positive support of this plan is found in Town of Cody records. Dr. Chamberlin applied to Cody City Council for permission to build a brick and stone building on Lot 10 of Block 50, and permission was granted on October 4,1909, according to Cody town council minutes, page 87. His moving out of the main building would free up one or two rooms to rent out.

When the buildings were brought from Wiley Town in Oregon Basin into Cody, the one placed on the south east corner of the 1000 block, Sheridan Avenue, in 1926, became the Trumbull Inn, which was later called the Green Gables, with rooms and a restaurant. In 2003, it became Maxwell's, a restaurant with no rentals.

By Agnes Chamberlin word for word

CHAMBERLIN BOARDING HOUSE

Before the Chamberlin Hotel came the boarding house. The Chamberlins moved off Sheridan Avenue, (Main Street), around the corner to 12th Street in the spring of 1904. This was at the time when Hud Darrah furnished the lumber and built the core of the complex, a framed two story dwelling which is pictured in the Wyoming Industrial Journal of 1906 as being the dental parlor and residence of Dr. Chamberlin. In this new building Agnes had three bedrooms to rent.

Back in 1905 Agnes started her boarding house in her new quarters with two tables full in the dining room. With the Bureau of Reclamation working on the Shoshone and Corbett dam projects and the Sulphur Mills starting up in January of 1906, business boomed. Sulphur was mined and shipped out for use in making paper and sheep dip.

Recent photo of the Duplex that was the original court house for Cody
Picture by Jo Jean DeHony

The clue to when Mark built his dental office is found in Town of Cody records. Dr. Chamberlin applied to Cody City Council for permission to build a brick and stone building on lot 10 of block 50, and permission was granted on October 4th, 1909, according to Cody town council minutes. His moving out of the main building would free up one or two rooms to rent out.

A collection of so many writings by Agnes Chamberlin was found in the hotel, or given to Jo Jean by a Cody Resident who thought it necessary for her to have them and have them rewritten for people to read and enjoy. They are retyped in the exact words and layout as the original written by Agnes

BY ESTER JOHANSSON MURRAY

Agnes' sister, Bertha Brown, lived with her from 1903-1912. Bertha later married and moved away, but in 1905 both ladies came into a handsome inheritance and immediately began to consider possible investments. Besides investing in the flour mill, Agnes bought a farm east of Cody and struggled with renters and scanty returns until she sold it in 1916, which gave her some hard cash for building her new hotel in the spring of 1917.

Her happiest and most successful accomplishment was her hotel. She had gained valuable experience from her boarding house and she was financially able at this point to embark on the new venture.

The 28th of March of 1917, she temporarily moved into empty space across the street in the grey sandstone Walls Building and construction began on her new hotel. Her contractors were Algott Johnson and Bill Rankin. Algott Johnson emigrated from Sweden in 1894, and in 1905 moved to Cody, joining many other Swedes already here. William Rankin, although born in Effington, Illinois, moved to Cody from Oregon in 1908.

The contractors first moved the false front, frame building to the back and dug a basement in the front for the new hotel. While Agnes and her long-time assistant, Mabel Watson temporarily lived across the street, they set to work sewing sheets and pillow cases for the hotel and cotton house dresses for themselves.

We can get an idea of the lobby from old photographs which shows her piano on the east side, and on the south side, the wide, well built, brick fireplace with a mounted elk head above it. A small desk and many chairs complete the furnishings. The floor is pictured uncarpeted.

In the 1917 new kitchen, the builders installed a large cement slab on which Agnes' new double oven Majestic cook stove stood and behind the stove, tin sheeting on the wall gave fire protection. Her large dining room was on the north side.

The new hotel was barely finished, when in 1918, Agnes invested $8000 in adding more rooms. When she opened her new dining room on the northeast side she had room to seat twenty-four at five tables and business boomed because she and Mabel had reputations of being fabulous cooks. Her clientele consisted mainly of the young business men, mostly bachelors. She started serving meals on a professional scale when Mabel Watson came to work for her on January 1, 1910, and she closed her popular dining room in 1920 and turned the space into several bedrooms. Another change came when she transformed the old barn into an annex. After World War One came a depression and her business.

Everyone liked the home cooked meals. People went to the Chamberlin for Sunday dinner. Cody and Meeteetse people. Meals were served individually. You had three choices usually. There were two long tables and two smaller ones. One of the tables was called the Home Table and that's where the bachlors in town and Doc Chamberlin would eat. The food at the tables was served home style.

HOTEL CHAMBERLIN REGISTER

While The Irma Hotel always held the rank of premier hotel on Cody's main street, Hotel Chamberlin had loyal followers through the years so that the same names appear over and over and it had its share of the rich and famous. The registers for this research date back only to August 1, 1917, when on this opening date of her new hotel, a brand new, big, black register graced her counter. It was the first of twelve volumes Jo Jean DeHony was able to provide the price of rooms and "if with bath" there was an extra charge. Agnes charged 75 cents per meal.

Some names appear frequently for long spells and then disappear such as the Altbergers from South Fork who sold their ranch to J. C. Nichols; and the W. A. Betts from Belknap Ranch who sold to Calvin Case. All the residents from Upper South Fork gave Valley as their residence even if they lived miles above or below Valley, the location of their post office. From the middle area they listed Ishawooa, the name of that area's post office. The fifty mile North Fork proved closer and more accessible to Cody, so there are fewer names of ranchers from there, who could make the trip in one day. However, we find W. H. Howell from Holm Lodge one of the most frequent renters and often at the same time his business partner Miss Shawver. Unkind gossip linked their names romantically, but Billy Howell had already experienced one marriage and had a good friend, Jo Hall who worked in Cody. They both favored brown and white pinto horses. It is highly unlikely Billy and Miss Shawver had a liaison, even a discreet one, although Mrs. Kate Buckingham claimed they did. All through the years they registered with separate rooms at the Hotel Chamberlin. After her retirement, Miss Shawver wrote a 93 page book of her memoirs called, *Sincerely, Miss S*. She used letter format and included several photographs. In the frontispiece, she used a photo of Billy Howell, on his pinto, Navaho, waving his cowboy hat. Miss Shawver greatly admired her business partner.

The first notable names in the 1917 register were: Kate Whitney from Meeteetse, wife of Fred Whitney, said to be the "poor relation" of the New York Whitneys; and David Dickie of the LU Ranch, from Dickie, Wyoming, between Meeteetse and Thermopolis, who stayed over in town. Dave is buried in his own mausoleum on a hill overlooking his ranch. Dave Dickie was said to be father of Anna Lucylle Moon (Hall). Anna Moon (1903-1993) was exposed to schooling to make her a finished gentlewoman, but she became the ultimate cowgirl. Ernest May registered from Lead, South Dakota. May later bought a ranch on the Wood River above Meeteetse. Mr. and Mrs. L. G. Phelps from Pitchfork signed the register. Phelps in 1906 bought the Pitchfork mortgages of Otto Franc, original owner, after Franc, died from an accidental gunshot in 1904.

The actress Elsie Ferguson (1883-1961) stayed at the Hotel on April 27, 1918, with her entourage. In 1909, she had played the heroine of *Pierre of the Plains* on Broadway and which was filmed under the title, *Heart of the Wilds*, in 1918, on locations near Cody: on the road to the Depot, on the east side of Canyon, and in the badlands north of Garland, Wyoming. Why Garland? Perhaps because the railroad ran close to picturesque eroded hills, thus equipment and horses could be transported easily.

ELSIE FERGUSON

Elsie Louise Ferguson was an American stage and film actress. Born in New York City, Elsie Ferguson was the only child of Mr. and Mrs. Hiram Benson Ferguson, a successful attorney. Raised and educated in Manhattan, she became interested in the theater at a young age and made her stage debut at seventeen as a chorus girl in a musical comedy. She quickly became known as one of the most beautiful women to ever set foot on the American stage. For almost two years from 1903-05 she was a cast member in The Girl from Kays which despite its title . . .

ELSIE FERGUSON NICKNAME "The Aristocrat of the Screen" Birth Name Elsie Louise Ferguson, born August 19, 1883, New York City, New York, USA, and Died November 15, 1961, in New London, Connecticut, USA. Height 5' 5".

The great Broadway stage actress and silent film star Elsie Louise Ferguson was born on August 19, 1883, in New York City, the only child of prominent lawyer Hiram Benson Ferguson and his wife. Due to her father's wealth, hers was a privileged childhood, though she developed a penchant for socialism in her late thirties.

Educated in Manhattan, Elsie made her theatrical debut as a chorus girl in the musical comedy "The Belle of New York" at the Madison Square Theatre in 1900. Her early flirtation with the stage was linked to a friend importuning her to join the chorus, which she did out of curiosity. She also was a chorus girl in

"The Liberty Belles" the following year. Allowed to speak one line in "Belles", she made up her mind to become a stage actress. Elsie was quite beautiful, as well as talented, and she worked her way up from the chorus to become a Broadway star for three decades. She made her Broadway debut, proper, at the end of 1903 in the musical "The Girl from Kay's" at the Herald Square Theatre, in 1 904, she then appeared in the play "The Second Fiddle."

Paramount managed to sign Elsie to a two-year, four-picture contract in late 1921, and she filmed a movie version of her stage success, "Sacred and Profane Love" (1921), with director by William Desmond Taylor, a man who himself would fall victim to a bullet at the beginning of 1921, as had Stanford White almost two decades earlier. Supporting player Maxine Elliott Hicks, who described her leading lady in "Love" as 'ritzy' in a 1990 interview, said, "She wouldn't allow anyone on the set, including Momma, but she was a darling to me."

Elsie's husband, Victor Egan, died in France in 1956. Widowed for five years, Elsie died at the age of 78 on November 15, 1961. With no surviving heirs, she left $1,000,000 to New York City's Animal Medical Center.

None of Elsie Ferguson's silent films are known to exist, although a 35mm print of "Forever" (1922) that had been owned by Dorothy Davenport Reid, Wallace Reid's widow, may have made it into the hands of a private collector. Her sole talkie, "Scarlet Pages," does exist and is part of the Time-Warner library of films. It occasionally is shown by the cable movie network Turner Classic Movies and remains the sole legacy of this great actress' spectacular career in the first part of the last century.

We now continue Writings of Ester
Johannson Murray.

Early guests, the J. R. Painters from Painter, Wy, came in from their Upper Sunlight ranch. Mr. Painter and Caroline Lockhart became romantically involved for awhile. He gave Caroline an amethyst and diamond ring, but he later pulled out and left his family and started mining in the Salmon River Canyon of Idaho. First Sunlight Ranger, John Rollinson fell in love with young Marguerite Painter, but his marital state made him unacceptable and he moved to California. She later married Ed Heald.

Colonel A. A. Anderson, artist from New York, who owned the Palette Ranch on Upper Greybull, stayed in the hotel in 1918 and 1920, accompanied by daughter and granddaughter. Local gossips said he sometimes brought young women from New York to model. Supposedly they posed naked, creek side on flat rocks, and neighbor cowboys spied on them with field glasses. How they stayed motionless despite hot sun, horse and deer flies and mosquitoes is a wonder. Not all his neighbors liked Colonel Anderson and the gossip was vicious. The men named the picturesque creek, Whorehouse Creek-later changed to Warhorse. Bill Bosler supplied this information in 2004. His mother had cooked for A. A. Anderson at the Palette Ranch.

On December 12, 1919, Agnes left a note on the register, "5, 6, 7, 8, 10 vacant—help yourself." And once during the summer of 1920, Agnes left the note: "Help yourself, I have gone to bed". Signed "A.B.C.".

By 1923 and1924, Barry Williams, listed Valley Post Office as his address, and lived up river on the Deer Creek Ranch. His sister, Hope Williams, had success as a New York actress.

Mr. and Mrs. Westerman (Henry and Retta), who worked for Col. Little of The Flying H Ranch, stayed at the Chamberlin when they came to town. They later worked for George Heald, then for N. P. deMauriac and at Coe Lodge. From Thermopolis, on January 14, 1924, W. L. Simpson and young son, Milward Simpson, visited Cody and signed in. E. V. Robertson from the Hoodoo and W. R. Coe from Coe Lodge were guests. L. H. Larom from Valley, Wyoming signed in on May 7, 1924. No names appear oftener through the years than Mr. and Mrs.L. H. Larom, who faithfully stayed at Hotel Chamberlin, favoring room 18, and continued when it was called the Pawnee Hotel. Jo Jean DeHony rented to the Laroms until 1974 or so. Larry Larom's nephew, Henry Larom and wife came to Valley in the early thirties. Henry, who became a fairly successful western writer of stories for youths, followed his uncle's choice of hotel. And Mrs. Walter Larom, the well-liked "Aunt Carrie", who built a home just below Valley, also preferred Hotel Chamberlin.

Mrs. Carl Johansson rented a room October 8, 1921; she was working for the Rumseys at Blackwater Camp. Carl Bloom, who was living in Casper, came to Cody on business and rented on December 23, 1924. Bloom survived an accident while working as a carpenter on a multi-story building in Denver. The wind blew him off a six-inch beam he was crossing on the sixth story. He landed on the ceiling of the first floor and sustained a broken nose. June 11, 1927, Carl J. Johansson chose to stay in town at the hotel instead of traveling three miles to stay with his brothers on the farm.

The H. T. Newells, who in the early days worked at the Palette and Pitchfork ranches, often stayed at the Hotel, but later became managers of the Irma Hotel. W. O. Sanzenbacher from Sunlight area and Ernest May from the Wood River on the opposite side of Park County, became faithful visitors and these two friends of Agnes, years later were pall bearers at her funeral. Senator Warren from Cheyenne stayed at the Chamberlin when he campaigned in Park County, October 18, 1920.

Perhaps the most famous celebrity to sign Agnes' register was Ernest Hemingway from Key West, Florida, who stayed in room 18, on October 16, 1932. He hunted with Lawrence Nordquist of the L Bar T Ranch on the upper Clarks Fork. Hemingway, a Nobel laureate, later resided permanently in Ketchum, Idaho, and shot himself there July 2, 1961.

Inserted from history found in Archives

STAYED AT THE CHAMBERLIN IN ROOM #18 ON OCTOBER 16, 1932

ERNEST MILLER HEMINGWAY was an American author and journalist. His economical and understated style had a strong influence on 20th-century fiction.

Lived: Jul 21, 1899-Jul 02, 1961 (age 61)

Height: 6' (1.83 m)

Spouse: (2)

Children: 3)

In 2001, two of his books, The Sun Also Rises and A Farewell to Arms, would be named to the list of the 100 best English-language novels of the 20th century by the editorial board of the American Modern Library.

Chaotic life. Fifty-one years later, he used a gun to kill himself. He was a tough, strong man with strong principles. Hemingway "believed that life was a tragedy and knew it could only have one end", yet he was blessed with talent and drive.

That may have made it harder for him to admit his failures and correct them.

In A Farewell to Arms it is mainly human commitment, and in For that makes the theme stand out sharply, and that's why it is difficult to analyze it.

No matter what exactly happens in those two books, violence and death and experiences area man's problems. They only had an abstract ideal they knew from his book peasant, as strong as a buffalo. A sportsman. And ready to live the life he writes about. He would never have it if his body had not allowed him to live it. But giants of his sort are truly modest; there is much more behind Hemingway's form than people know."

In 1918 he left the Star to travel overseas. Against his father's wishes, he tried to join the United States Army but failed the medical examination. Later, he enlisted in the Ambulance Corps and left for Italy.

On July 8, 1918, at the Italian front he was wounded by machine gun fire, ending his career as an ambulance driver. After being discharged from the Army, Hemingway returned home and in 1920 took a job in Toronto, Ontario, Canada at the Toronto Star newspaper as a freelancer, staff writer, and foreign correspondent.

Bohlin, of Hollywood, California, stayed on August 17, 1934, after he became famous for his silver-mounted leather saddles. Some of his work is now displayed in the Buffalo Bill Historical Center. He created over 12,000 saddles during his career. (Before he became famous, he was known in Cody, as that young Swedish fellow called Eddie). His Cody shop was across the street from the Irma Hotel, according to an early Cody newspaper. He married Harriet Sweem in Cody, November 19, 1920, and died in Los Angeles at age 85. The elder Lloyd Taggart of Cody bought one of Bohlin's luxury saddles.

A couple times, J. A. Smith signed in, and under "residence" wrote, "Wings of the Morning". Most of the time it was the steady visits of traveling salesmen who repeatedly signed the register.

Clyde Johnson, the Christian Science practitioner from Sheridan whom Agnes claimed helped her so much, stayed often over the years from 1925 through the 1930's. Agnes furnished him a complimentary room. Agnes seldom favored anyone with a complimentary room except Clyde and other Christian Scientists in his party from Sheridan. However on March 30, 1936, Mrs. M. 1. Allen stayed free. Mary Jester Allen ran the Cody Museum, a project dear to Agnes' heart.

Lawrence Tenney Stevens, a notable western sculptor, had first come west from Bedford, New York, to visit on the deMauriac ranch on North Fork. Some wags thought maybe "Steve" had been invited to the ranch as a possible suitor for the deMauriac's daughter, Alice. Later, Stevens married, and he and his wife and her three daughters motored west on a honeymoon. They paid a visit to the deMauriacs, and stayed on a South Fork dude ranch. They bought Mrs. Kaufman's Double L Bar ranch. On June 21, 1936, L. T. Stevens registered from Dallas, Texas. As of 2004 one of his step-daughters, "Roz" Siggins, still lives in Cody. On October 17, 1935, Ann Austin and Ruby Davies from the upper South Fork registered. They probably were stopping over in town on their way East to spend the winter at Ann's eastern home, "Rosemont Estate" in Pennsylvania. Ann bought the Hubner Place where they spent their summers. The Austin family wealth came from railroads and her sister married into the DuPont family. Ruby was daughter of John Reckless Daviss, original owner of the farthest ranch up the South Fork, the present Majo Ranch. Ruby worked as a dude wrangler on the Aldrich dude ranch where Ann was a "dudine" in the 1920's. Ann and Ruby became life long friends.

On August 15, 1939, R. K. Davies from Ishawooa signed into room 2, and A. A. Austin had the famous room #18.

On December 31, 1938, Agnes wrote in the register, "The only night in over twenty-one years in which there was not one guest in the house."

During the Depression years, there were fewer tourists in the summer, but always a steady business of traveling salesmen. During the 1930's the Sunlight and Crandall area began to be developed and because of the distance, a great increase in names from there were registered to Hotel Chamberlin: Lawrence and Olive Nordquist from the L Bar T ranch, and their dude wranglers, Ivan Wallace and Chuck Weaver. Johnny McGrew, forest ranger from the area went off to fight in World War II and won the Purple Heart in the Battle in New Guinea. He never could pull himself together afterwards, a casualty of the war.

Johnny Kirkpatrick stayed over the 4th of July, 1937, probably because of being involved with the Cody Stampede and parade. Johnny was the ultimate prototype Texas cowboy. He came to Wyoming in 1902, having ridden north with the last cattle herd on the Chisholm Trail. He died in August 1948, at the age of 80, after actively cowboying into his late 70's.

CHAMBERLIN-PAWNEE HOTEL

The long progression in upgrading their dwelling from the frame house they built on the large property they bought between Sheridan and Rumsey Avenues, (about a sixth of a town block), until the big project of the 1917 hotel, is difficult to follow. The present Pawnee Hotel gives the appearance of one large unit, but inside there have been alterations and additions too numerous to untangle. In 1939 Agnes sold her hotel to Hattie and George Edwards; and in 1941 they changed the name to Pawnee. In 1974, Jo Jean DeHony bought it and began remodeling and upgrading. In February of 2003, present owner, Jo Jean, cheerfully provided a guided tour of the upstairs and downstairs, pointing out where tasteful wallpaper covers old brick partitions. In the eighteen original rooms, somewhat altered from the 1917 construction, are original windows, corner sinks, and radiators.

Stairs in Pawnee Hotel during Jo Jean's Ownership
Photo by Jo Jean DeHony

The original stairway to the second floor of the hotel is still in use. In the lower hallway are the original three-pronged coat hooks and the looped fire hose, attached to a water faucet. The original fifty feet of two-inch wide hose is still neatly folded in a rack that can be swung outward from the wall. A fifteen-inch Asian dagger, possibly of Philippine origin, had been hidden behind the folded fire hose in its swing-out bracket. The handle consisted of an open-mouth monkey face, and the narrow, eleven-inch blade fitted into a hand-made leather sheath. This, a well-sharpened, deadly weapon, has a story yet to be revealed.

In the front office is the red brick fireplace with its wide four-foot opening, so well constructed it still draws nicely according to the present owner. A small telephone exchange with twenty connections is kept as a memento. Whether or not Agnes had room telephones installed is not known. Still in use in the front vestibule are three dark brown doors, each with twelve panels of beveled glass.

Agnes ended up with eighteen rooms. Jo Jean DeHony now has twenty two rooms to rent.

From the upper hallway there was access to an attic where Jo Jean found old memorabilia stored, including glass photo plates which Jo Jean had developed; they were of Indians, so far unidentified as to tribe.

WE ARE NOW ABLE TO READ AND APPRECIATE MORE OF THE ACTUAL WRITINGS BY AGNES CHAMBERLIN

THE HOTEL CHAMBERLIN

By Agnes Chamberlin

In spite of Algot Johnson thinking the building would cost me too much, I started in about the 28th of March. We moved into the Walls building and had just gotten the old house moved back, the basement half dug and the whole place torn up when it began to storm. It snowed and turned cold and it looked hopeless, but there was nothing to do but go forward. I am always undertaking projects that are in advance of my understanding, so it is always doubly hard for me to go through with them. All during the spring and the ups and downs of building, I was at times terribly beset by aggressive mental suggestion and did not know what it was or how to handle it. I would go to the picture show in good spirits, but pretty soon the thought would overwhelm me, "why did I ever think I could carry through such a big job as I had undertaken." It would seem to me that I would pass out with terror and self-depreciation. But the next morning I would fly at it with renewed energy and courage. One day Mrs. Van Horn nearly floored me by saying that "the men," which meant Mr. Van Horn, said I could not succeed in the hotel business because I was so unfitted for it by temperament. That was a body blow, but the word was "forward," and forward

I went. During the spring one day Mabel and I went over to Billings to hear Booker T. Washington speak. He was one of the most absorbingly interesting speakers I ever heard, and while he spoke two hours, I could have listened to him for two hours more. He was so simple, clear and earnest that no one could help being impressed by him.

When the new equipment for the hotel began to arrive, it was very interesting. In February, before I had let the contract for my house, I had ordered my silver and linens, and both were very nice and some of them are still in use. I also ordered my two-oven Majestic range from Van Arsdale in February. When this range came and was set up in my little kitchen I had a panic, for I thought it would break me feeding so much coal into it. As a matter of fact, it took no more coal than the nice 6-hole Majestic I had used for fifteen years and it has been a joy forever in my work. On June 28th while the new part of the house was still unplastered, I opened up for business in the dining room and the four rooms in the old part that were finished. I had four traveling men the first night and all the rest of that year and the next, while the war was on, my house was full and running over and I had crowds in my dining room. I look back sometimes and thank God that He gave me the strength to work as I did and prospered me in it.

Those days I kept a cow that had to be fed and milked, but I usually got Mark to milk for me. In the winter I would have a high-school boy to stoke the furnace and take care of the cow, but in the summer I took care of feeding her and even milked when Mark was unavailable. Many and many a morning that first summer I would get up at 4:30 and go with my little Saxon car out along the roadsides or the park and cut green feed for my cow before I started in to get breakfast for from twenty-five to fifty people. There were tourist those days, and also being war times there were lots of salesmen, geologists, relief workers, ranchers and everybody on the move. Roads and cars were not as good then as they are now, and when Mrs. Rumsey came down from Blackwater or people came from Meeteetse or Basin or even Powell, they would stay overnight. Mr. Larom was just starting in on the Valley Ranch and he would be in town a lot, only he always stayed at Dew's Irma's mothers. I would see him driving around proudly in his old Cadillac and think he was very high hat. Mark was spending all his time at his ranch and kept a team for the purpose, all of which irritated me immeasurably. The building of the hotel separate Mark and me for good as far as having anything in common went. I had been longing for years for something to separate us without making a nasty scandal, so when I started to build this hotel and moved Mark's bed into the back of the office building and I slept in my little room where I have been ever since, that completed the separation as far as I was concerned. I don't think Mark cared much, although he was of a disposition to be more attached to a wife than I was to a husband. I always had to get the consent of my reason for everything, and Mark went by his feelings. We got along nicely when we were first married, but as time went on and I got into my stride in business and intellectual pursuits we got farther and farther apart. He was not intellectual, but enjoyed hunting and fishing and playing chess, of the later of he became very expert through years of mis-spent time. I used to have to hunt all over town for him when a patient would come, and at last find him playing chess somewhere and perhaps he would send word to the patient that he was busy and would be at the office after awhile. He was the same way about Hunting and fishing when we first came here. He would go off and say he would be only two or three days, but it would be two weeks before he would show up. People would come in for fifty miles on horseback with an aching tooth, only to find him gone and no other dentist in town. I got so when he was out hunting I would not go to the door when anybody knocked, because I was so ashamed to have to tell them that he was gone and I had no idea when he would be back. As he got more and more absorbed in chess, he quit hunting so much and soon took up ranching instead. It was always some expensive fad that took him away from his business. I was ambitious and industrious and wanted to get ahead, so that this happy-go-lucky attitude of Mark's galled me terribly and I got so I despised him for being such a sucker and letting everything and everybody that was of no account, work him. I was so busy with my own plans and ambitions that I overlooked the fact that I should be kind and courteous to Mark. He was a good man, as men go, kind and courteous and fairly honest, when self-interest did not prompt him to be otherwise. People liked him and thought I was hard on him, which I now admit that I was, but that is all over now and I am sorry and have learned to appreciate his good qualities and be sorry that I was not nicer to him. However, I am not a marrying woman and would never think of marrying again. I suppose that if I had never married, I would think I had missed something, but now I know marriage is not for women like me, for they don't give the job the attention and serious thought that it deserves. I would never have had the chance for development that my marriage to Mark gave me, for I was too timid and negative in my thinking to ever overcome the obstacles that beset my environment in Kansas, and I would never have had the gumption to get away from there and carve out a career for myself. I went to Wyoming when I was younger, but had not the qualities of character to make a go of it. Also I went to Oklahoma, but had bogged down there just as I would have done anywhere else. It was only through my marriage to Mark and the stiffening of my moral fiber that his ineffectiveness compelled me to acquire that I was able to force myself ahead and make a success of my little business and what is more important of myself.

THE WAR

Mother was very intelligent and sympathetic and a very good raconteur. She was always homesick for Illinois and her people and spent many hours telling Bertha and me, as well as friends, about happenings in her youth and before she came to Kansas. One of the things she was eloquent about was the Civil War end the part she and her relatives and friends played in it. From her we learned all about the hardships of war, the devotion and patriotism of those who stayed at home and worked for the war while their men-folks fought, the horrors of Anderson and Libby prisons and all the rest of the horrid mess. Since I had grown up I had read much of the propaganda for peace and against war, and I believed so thoroughly in the power and lasting qualities of our modern civilization that I often said that a great war was impossible in the modern world. When war began in Europe in 1914 I didn't believe it for months. It did not seem possible that such a thing could happen in a Christian world. As year after year of it dragged along I became convinced that there was a European war, but was so sure, with all other western people, that the United States would not get into it. All the winter of 1916-17 people from the east who had business here would tell us that we had no idea how close we were to war, and that we were bound to get into it. I would not listen to such predictions, and as I had decided to build my hotel in the spring, I went right on with my plans. If I had believed that this country was going into the war, I would not have dared to start building, but it was fortunate for me that I did not know what was coming, or I would have held back and never achieved the success I have now. It was a terribly cold winter and the 28th of March was the first warm, pleasant day we had since the first of the year. That evening Algot Johnson and Bill Rankin came to bring me their estimate on the cost of my building. Algot said, "it is too high and you won't build it." I said I had to build, for I was crowded out of my present space and could not let this opportunity pass. So I signed the contract then and there and the next day operations began. We moved across the street into Judge Walls' building and there Mabel and I sewed and hemmed sheets and pillowcases and made housedresses for three months. Archer and Judge Walls boarded with us and aside from getting meals; we worked on equipment for the new house all the time. On April 7th war was declared and the high schoolboys began leaving school to enlist and I thought I could not endure it. The first boys to go went to the artillery, to the navy and to aviation. Then the militia company from Cody filled out its organization and went away. All the coming year groups of young men were leaving in bunches or singly and the town was going to the depot to see them off. I never went to see any of them off, for I knew I would go all to pieces if I did and I couldn't bear it. When Mrs. Tinkcom's only son went it was the worst. Many and many a time I thought in agony, "what can I say to Mrs. Tinkcom when her boy fails to come back?" The war hysteria was upon all of us, and what with standing over the hot stove for long hours every day, saving sugar and hearing people kick about it, trying to bake with the four substitutes, saving to buy bonds and saving stamps and worrying over the boys who would never come back, it was the hardest year I ever put in. The first year I saw an article in a Denver paper by a French woman in Denver telling about a letter she had from a French mother asking her if she couldn't find a god-mother for her son who, was a prisoner in Germany. I wrote Mille. Paggi at once and offered to do all I could for this young man. She put me into communication with the French Red Cross, and until after the armistice I sent Ten Dollars a month to France for rations for Jean Joffin. Soon after I took up Jean I also adopted his brother Emile, who was in the army near Belgium somewhere. Emile and his mother wrote to me in French and I would send their letters together with my replies to Mlle. Paggi to translate. This all kept me busy and interested as long as the war lasted. At Christmas time I sent each of the boys a carton of cigarettes, as well as other little luxuries. Mrs. Russell Crane knitted a pair of sox for each of them, and it was all very interesting and kept up my spirits. I had all along the hope that when the war was over one or more of the Joffin boys would be so disgusted with France that they would come over here and learn my business and be a help to me, but that was a vain hope. As soon as the war was over Emile married. Afterwards he wrote me and wanted to come to me, but I would not have him because he was married and I couldn't be burdened with a family. He was cad enough to offer to leave his wife behind if I would only let him come. Of course that Mille Paggi was a trump and she had a friend whose husband was a chef at a veterans' hospital near Paris. There was a young man there, an assistant cook, who thought he would like to come to America. I was already to make arrangements for him to come when he backed out. Mille Paggi said her friend said he was often very sorry he did not come, for things went badly with everybody in France after that was, as everybody knows. Also Mille Paggi's suggestion I sent the money for her friend to go out to Charleville and look up the Joffins after Emile wanted to come to me. She made the long, disagreeable journey for me and returned a true bill on the whole outfit. She saw Jean as he passed by the hotel, but he was so trampish that she did not speak to him. The hotel woman told her they were no good, even before the war, owing bills everywhere and being lazy and bad. Jean only wrote me one letter after he returned from being a prisoner in Germany. I wrote right back and asked him to tell me all about it, but he never did. I would have been so glad to have those boys come over here and help me and done well by them, for the help situation was dreadful after the war. No one would do housework and Mabel and I worked our-selves almost to death. But it was not to be, and I suppose it was all for the best.

When Armistice Day came it was not the thrill I had expected it to be, for we had had the "false Armistice" the Thursday before and that took all the joy out of the real armistice. However, it was with a great feeling of relief that I stopped at once using substitute flour and quit parceling out the sugar and using honey for pies and puddings.

CHAPTER 15

ADDED MORE ROOMS, BOUGHT CAR AND TRIP TO CALIFORNIA

ALL THROUGH THE war business was humming. My rooms were filled every night and I had all the people I could possibly cook for every meal. I got 75 cents a meal straight through, even for breakfast. When I opened the house there were still many things lacking to make it complete, but there was a mortgage on it of $8,000 and a floating debt of about Two Thousand. It was fortunate for me that business was good, for by the first of the next May I had bought many things for the house out of the income and had also paid off all of the unsecured debts. Along in May I brought a smile to Mr. Parks' face by coming in and paying the first Five Hundred Dollar payment on my mortgage. I received Two or Three Thousand from Aunt Jennie's estate in the next two or three years and of course all that went into paying off the mortgage. I built in 1917 and by the spring of 1920 I had all my debts paid, took a trip to California to visit my father whom I had not seen for twenty years and when I came back I bought me an Oldsmobile touring car for almost $1800.00. Then I closed my dining room and worked over the rest of the old part of the house and added some more rooms to the tune of another $8000.00. This was a bad move, for right after the war prices were high and this building cost me much more than it was worth. The bottom fell out of business just then and I was no longer in getting this building project paid for than I was the first. Eventually it was paid for and then the oil boom came along and I needed more room. Then I finished up the house as it now stands and re-opened my dining room. I kept that open until after the depression got well under way, when I leased it to a woman who made a failure of it. That gave me the excuse I long had wanted of closing the dining room forever. It got so that people would not eat in a dining room. They would sit on a stool in a restaurant and have sinkers and coffee for a meal, or else they would buy some rolls and a bottle of milk and sit in their car and eat them.

Mrs. Agnes Chamberlin in California

Collection of Jo Jean DeHony

However, I did well with the new building and the dining room as long as the oil boom lasted. I got the building all paid for and also moved the old barn around and made it into an annex, which made good money until the oil boom broke. I got entirely out of debt at this time and had quite a sum of money invested in securities. One year I paid income tax on over Six Thousand Dollars net profit. In the meantime I bought the lot west of Mrs. Pool's and began to improve it for a home to retire to when I had made enough money. I spent a lot of money on that and then last year sold it for half what I paid out on it. The depression put a stop to my making any clear money for seven years, I was getting older and the object in having a home like that which I would be too old to enjoy or keep up properly seemed so remote that when Mrs. Donely wanted the lot I just let it go for what it was worth to her. In addition to not saving anything for the last seven years, I have cashed in on a lot of securities and used the money on improving the house and buying me a new car. I had when the depression started almost Twenty Thousand Dollars in securities, including what my Building and Loan stock would be worth when I cashed in on it. Now my Building and Loan stock will all be forced out by the first of next year and I have lost some of my investments and my farm in Kansas don't bring in anything except the taxes. At this time all my securities and the farm together will not be worth more than Ten Thousand Dollars when the stocks come back to par. The depression has taught me a lot about values, and I am not putting my income and Building and Loan stock into real values, which will not perish in any depression. This is giving me more satisfaction than the saving of money ever did and I know I am on the right track at last. Business has been better this year than for five years. We have fewer who do not haggle over the price and generally make themselves disagreeable. I have been able to put down some new carpets this spring and do other renovating of the place that is a great satisfaction. I have better health than I have had for

Hotel Chamberlin Lobby with the large Elk head and the fire place in the background. The piano is behind Agnes and the desk is to the right of her Collection of Jo Jean DeHony

Study my lessons thoroughly, go out some, read and listen to the radio, besides going places that I want to go. I have more peace of mind than I ever had before and the education and future success of my two boys gives me something to look forward to. I feel that life began at sixty-five for me, which is very late, but better late than never. The conquests over self that I complete here will not have to be repeated here after, so that I feel that all the good I can do here will be for eternity.

September 23, 1909 TAKEN FROM A NEWSPAPER PRINTING:

DR. CHAMBERLIN TO BUILD

Collection of Jo Jean DeHony

Two views of the Chamberlin Hotel, re-
produced from photographs in Mrs.
Chamberlin's scrapbook, now in the pos-
session of Margaret Hamlin. In the
photograph on the left, the original frame
building is visible with Doc Chamberlin's

Dr. M. Chamberlin, the well known dentist, has started the erection of a brick office building on a lot to the north of his present location. The building will be 20 x 20 and will be used exclusively by the Doctor and his associate for office purposes. The present combined office and residence will be used exclusively for residence purposes. The Doctor has always enjoyed a fine practice and we are glad to not his evidence of prosperity.

THE FARM

I had not had my money long when one day Houx, Mrs. Newell's father, who was prominent in politics and business here at that time, came in and wanted to take us down east of town to look at a very nice 80-acre farm that the owner was anxious to sell and go back east to go into business with his brother-in-law. The upshot was that we went and bought the farm. Then I was in for it right. There was a team and a cow and some chickens to dispose of. One horse of the team was good and the other was not. They were sold separately and for not enough money. Mark and I made two trips down there and caught the chickens and brought them to town, where we fed them and sold them off as fast as they were big enough. I got a man to go down there and finish the crop and from then on for several years, I rented the farm to some neighbors. Of course I never made anything more than taxes off of it, and renters and neighbors stole my stuff off of it. Finally in 1912, when I made up my mind to go at things right and make some money, I took over the farm myself and hired a man to work it. I bought machinery and cattle and built onto the house and put up some barns and sheds out of lumber that I bought cheap from the old buildings at Corbett that the government had put up during the building of the Corbett tunnel. In all I spend $3,500 on the place and never made half enough off of it to pay back what I had borrowed. In the winter of 1916 I sold the farm, after holding it ten years, for just what I paid for it, with all the improvements and endless trips down there and the worry thrown in. However, I got the cash for it and it gave me a good start towards building my hotel in the spring of 1917. Thus endeth the farming episode. The last unpleasantness about the farm was very upsetting. When I sold in the fall I agreed to give possession the first of January, so the fellow from Nebraska who bought it came out here in October. He rented a house in town and camped down to wait for the first of January. When that date approached, he sent me notice that he wanted the place on that date. I told my renter to get off, but he refused to do so until in February, although he had known all along that he was expected to move then. But his wife was going to have another baby, she only had six then, and he refused to move. The buyer went to every lawyer in town and to one in Powell to try to sue me, but there was not one of them who would take the case. That was the first time in my life that I had an inkling that anybody respected me or would do anything to favor me. It was very sheering to my wounded spirits. Mrs. Crowe, a practitioner from Billings was staying here at my house while she worked for a patient in the country, and she worked for me thorough this crisis. I was never more upset about anything than about this. However, the buyer had to pipe down and I believe I gave him a hundred dollars, and my renter got out as soon as his wife got up after her confinement.

CHICKENS

Before I started to keep boarders, I thought maybe I could make something out of chickens. Accordingly I put up pens and built little houses all over the quarter of a block north of the house and sent away for my breeding stock. I fooled with chickens for two or three years before I saw that it was of no use and quit it. In that way I "learned about chickens from them." After the mill went to pot I kept casting around for some kind of business or profession to go into that would be interesting and profitable as well. Mark wanted me to go into the dental office with him, but I hated it and did not want to be under his thumb anyway. I could not think of anything that suited me and spent lots of anxious hours trying to figure out some way to occupy my time and make money, but never came to any conclusion.

THE BANK

I almost forgot to tell about my banking experience. About the time I was putting money into every shell game in the country, Frank Williams, who had been cashier at the Shoshoni National Bank, lost his job and proceeded to organize a new bank, a state bank, which was so much easier to do than a National bank. Of course Mark was all for it and Bertha and I each put a Thousand Dollars in stock in it. It ran a little over a year and then folded up and quit. It cost Frank's father almost all he had to keep Frank out of the pen for some of his transactions. He got Bertha to loan him Twelve Hundred Dollars on his homestead and she had to take it when he blew up and left the country. We got back about fifty percent of our money and had a very unpleasant experience.

MARK'S RANCH

When I inherited money Mark went completely wild and thought we were rich and must do all sorts of things. I never got excited about money and what we inherited did not seem like so much to me, although if we were careful it might have put us on easy street. But Mark wanted to get into everything and make a big splash and show off with it. I tried to get him to let me put my money into securities and let the interest compound for our nest egg for our old age, then live off of his profession. He thought working at dentistry was slow business, when one could make so much money off of land and businesses in this small town. For years he taunted me because I would not let him pay a Hundred Dollars an acre for a forty just east of town, because it was going to increase in value. That same land has never been worth $100 an acre not will it ever be. Finally one day I told him I never wanted to hear anything more about buying land, for I was not going to do it. Then one day when he was telling about how foolish it was for me to be unwilling to put money in some other sure thing around town, I told him with all the emphasis I was capable of that if he ever mentioned my putting money into anything again I would run off. I must have convinced him of my sincerity, for he never again asked me to put money into anything.

Along about 1910 a silly eye doctor from Sheridan was over here and he told us all about his lovely cabin in the mountains near Sheridan and told Mark he ought to have a mountain resort where he could go and hunt and fish and stay week-ends. That fit right in with Mark's ideas, so he proceeded to put it into practice. There was an old fellow up Trail Creek who had a "desert" claim and wanted to go to the soldiers' home, so Mark bought his relinquishment and proceeded at once to make expensive improvements on the place. He built a stone cabin out of the stone found there and put up a barn and plowed up ground to raise oats and alfalfa on and set endless trees and shruber and strawberry plants. I tried my best to disuade him from all this, but it was just like talking to the wind. He not only put in a lot of money up there trying to make a stock ranch out of it, but he spent more and more time there. He bought an old team and a buggy so as to make trips up there and he went there every Saturday afternoon and stayed until late Sunday night, working his head off, and the next spring people would let their sheep run in there and eat up everything he had planted. Every blessed Saturday my icebox and bread box were rifled for food to take up to "my ranch," and lots bought at the store besides. Then Sunday night after I had gone to bed I would hear the buggy rattle over the cross walk in the alley under my window and Mark would come into the kitchen and hunt up supper for himself. Then he would come upstairs and run him a bath and splash around in that for what seemed to me hours. Then he would proceed to open and shut drawers, getting his clean linen and underwear ready to put on in the morning. And all that time his electric light would be blazing away in my eyes and keep me from sleep. Oh, how I hated that ranch and how disgusted I got with Mark. It seemed to me that any fool would know better than to let a good profession go by the board while he fiddled around with a little place that would never bring him in a cent. Of course, man-like, he could not see it my way and went on to his doom with all the stubbornness and good humor of a perfectly irresponsible nice man. So that he might have more time to spend on his ranch, he went one summer to Denver and hired a young dentist from Denver University to come here and work in his office. The young man was not very experienced and some of Mark's patients did not like him very well, so in the end Mark lost business by it. At first there was lots of work and Mark proceeded to build a new office just north of the house. The office had always been in the front of the house before. He built this double office for two dentists and while it was being built he spent most of his time at his ranch. When it was done and moved into, he still put in a lot of time at the ranch, but somehow the office got paid for, and I never did understand how, with so much money going out and so little coming in. After about two years the business began to go on the rocks and the young dentist left and went to Basin, where he opened an office. Two years later, after he had married and had a baby he lost his mind and committed suicide one bright winter's morning. So ended the dental office expansion. After Mark died, I found that he had borrowed a lot of money on his ranch and nobody knew where it went to. I tried renting it, but could not get enough rent to pay the taxes and interest on the loan. The fences were falling down and would have to be replaced, neighbors were stealing everything movable off of it, Ed Heald would not let me have any water for the crop (the water right was just a flood right and therefore no good unless Ed Heald was willing to give it to me). I spent about two weeks figuring pro and con whether to keep the place and try to sell it some—day and get my money out of it, or to give it away. I figured that I would have to get Five Thousand Dollars for it within the next five years to come out even on it, and I did not believe it would ever be worth Five Thousand Dollars. A man had offered Mark $10,000 for it during the time he was alive and he wouldn't take it. He asked $12,000. I tried to get advice from Mr. Parks and he would not give me any, so I just followed my own judgement and one day went up town and offered to give it to Harry Sanborn. He took it and assumed all its debts and I washed my hands of it forever. Events since have proved that I was wise, for land has never been worth anything since.

MARK

When Mark brought his young assistant from Denver he had to board and room him. Bertha and I did not feel like doing so much work for nothing and so I began to look around for someone to do my housework. One day a girl who was working for Mrs. Simpson came in to have some dental work done and I asked her if she knew where I could get some help in the house. She had worked for Dr. Bennet's wife for seven years in Meeteetse and afterwards in Cody. She was a very fine looking girl and very nice, but I had never dreamed that she might come to work for me. I was delighted to get her, but could not take her until the office was finished, because I had no room for her to sleep in. So she came to me the first day of January, 1910, and has been with me ever since. When the young assistant left and I had no need for Mabel, I couldn't bear to see her leave, and as I had wanted for years to do something for myself instead of depending on Mark's erratic efforts for a living, I proceeded to take in a few boarders. Bertha was with me too, and between the three of us it went very well. I had my farming operations to see to and that with the boarders kept me very busy. I gradually got a nice crowd around me and we had a lot of nice times with the boys and girls who met here. This group was called by people all over town, "The Chamberlin Bachelors," and there was always some kind of high-jinks going on among them. Mabel, Bertha and I joined in on any fun there was and none of that group will ever forget the good times we had those days.

NOT MARRIED

One characteristic prank of the "Chamberlin Bachelors" was when Nova Brown, Mrs. Eoa C. Brown's husband, was going to take a party of girls from Vassar College out on a pack trip. There were to be about twenty of them and they were chaperoned by an old professor of the college. Their arrival was the subject of speculation at the table for days before they were to arrive. One day some bright mind suggested that the boys all go over and meet the Vassar Girls when they came in. This idea was at once hilariously adopted and preparations for the reception went forward without delay. Someone got some circles of white cardboard with the words, "Not Married," printed on them in large letters and each man wore one to the train. The news got out over town and several other young men, married and single came and wanted to join in the fun. So at last the great day came and when the train pulled into the station there stood about thirty men all lined up at the back of the platform wearing their badges. Nobody said a word, but they all just stood there. They said the girls would get off the train one at a time look up and see these men lined up and duck her head and giggle and run for the automobiles that were lined up to receive them. When it was all over and the girls gone, the boys came home well satisfied with their adventure.

Afterwards Nova Brown blew them up for it, saying that the old fussy professor was so indignant that he said he was never going to bring out another bunch of girls to be insulted. And he never did.

ALLEN MARRIED

Then Raymond Allen went back to Ohio and married Mrs. Allen, which was something more to be taken cognizance of. Preparations for the reception went on for days. A large wooden cage was built on the back of a truck and decorated with evergreen boughs, out of recognition of the forest service, the boys said. They all got ready to go and meet the train but somebody of the Allen's friends had seen Jake Schwoob and got him to go down to the Y with his car and get the Allens off of the train before it pulled into the station. Lady friends of the Allens had invaded the house where they were to live and gotten dinner well under way so that when they came Mary could finish it and the two newly-weds, could have their first dinner in their new home alone together. The train came in at noon and the gang was there with their truck and their cage to meet it. The word got around, however, that Jake was going to meet it at the Y, so, the boys got their truck squarely across the road coming from the depot to intercept them. When Jake came tearing along with his passengers and saw the obstruction, he just swerved to one side and passed them on one wheel and beat them to town. As soon as the boys got their truck turned around they came back to town too and went right to the Allen house. Of course they were denied admission, but one of them found a cellar window unfastened and crawled in and came upstairs and unfastened the kitchen door and let the rest of the gang in. They captured Allen and took him for a ride all over town and felt better.

Afterwards they rounded up Jake and put him in the cage and rolled him up street a short distance. They wanted to get hold of the cage, but Jake finally took it to the river and dumped it in. That ended the Allen reception.

MARK'S PARTY

Some of the local men whose wives were away and they took their meals at my house gave stage parties at their homes for my boys and a few others. So Mark thought he must give a party. It came off on commencement night of the high school. Mabel and I put the supper on the table and then went to commencement. Where it was held was in the building on Main Street that backs up just opposite our dining room windows. As we were listening to the young ideas being unfolded we could hear a faint roar from my dining room. After the supper was over Barber and Brady went over to Dew's, upstairs over the Home Supply store, and they sat on the back porch and watched people come up the street and hear the uproar and come down the alley and peer in the dining room windows to see what the racket was all about. When we got home, the crowd had all gone and the dining room was a wreck. One of the boys had been to Casper and gotten a nice looking cigar loaded with explosive, which he proceeded to put into Mark's box of cigars that he had gotten for his guests. When the crowd lighted up after supper Melton got the loaded cigar and when it went off the crowd went wild. Then Mark had to show them how proficient he was in standing on his head. He went to one side of the room and got his feet in the air when he lost his balance and fell right into Sanzie's lap. They both came down together with a crash, and that was what broke up the party. There was always something funny happening around my house and we all had lots of fun. As I look back at the bunch of gay youngsters I feel sad that so much sorrow and unhappiness has come to so many of them. Brady was divorced from his first wife and now is dead. Pauline Lantry married Sanzie and is dead. Harry Patton and Edith Judy were married and went to New Bern, N. C., to live and she was burned to death a few years ago. Barber married and lost his wife, married again and almost lost his mind. He lives in Washington some place now. Sanzie is getting old and is lonely and getting crabbed and "sot." Florence Gregory lost her first husband, but is happily married now and living in Grass Creek. Bob Gleeson lost his wife after his children were almost grown. Ted Hogg is dead. Fred Barnett lives in Peoria and is not very well. Mark has been dead for fourteen years now and Mabel has gotten very large and is not well most of the time.

Things went on this way until 1916 motorists began going through the Park and I got some of them for meals—I had no rooms to speak of. Bertha was married in the spring of 1912 and Mabel and I carried on alone. The Park business looked so good that I decided after a great deal of figuring and pondering about it that I could do well in a small hotel. People liked my cooking and I seemed to be fitted for that sort of thing. I began in the fall to draw plans, and along about Christmas my plans were mature enough to ask for bids on the building. It was one of the hardest winters we ever had here and it looked as though I would never get started on my work. At last I had things whipped into shape and the night of the 28th of March Algot Johnson came to bring me the estimate on the cost of building.

THE FOLLOWING PRICES FOR ROOMS IN THE HOTEL CHAMBERLIN WAS FOUND ON A PIECE OF STATIONARY FROM MRS. AGNES CHAMBERLIN

NO DATE WAS INDICATED

Rooms No, 1-3-4-5-12-20-21-22
$1.50 single, $2.00 double
Rooms 6 and   10 $1.50
       9 and   15 1.00

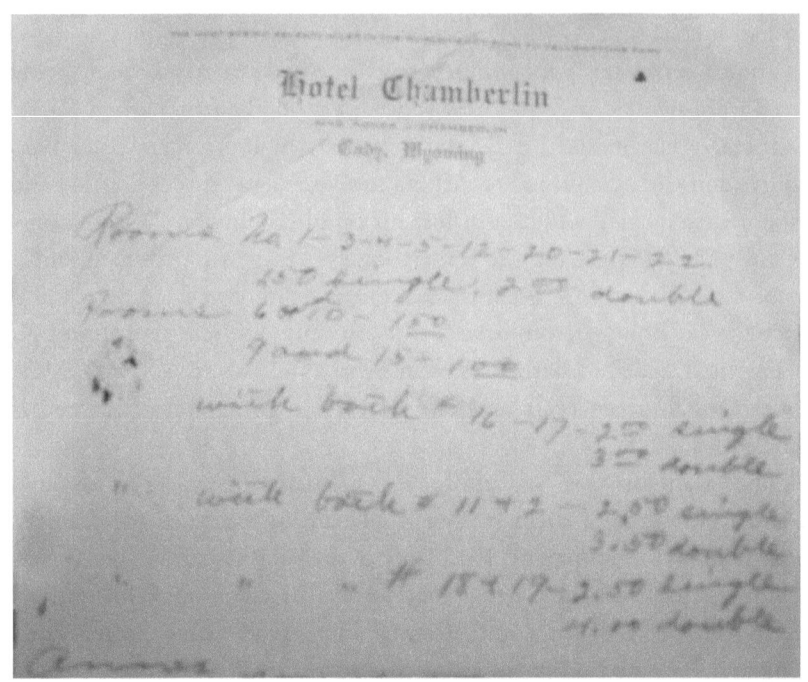

Property of Jo Jean DeHony

With bath #16-17   2.00 single
                           3.00 double

With bath #11 & 2   2.50 single
                           3.50 double

With bath #18 & 19   2.50 single
                           4.00 double

Annex rooms $1.50 single 2.00 double

ALONG WITH THIS PAPER WAS ANOTHER WITH THE FOLLOWING

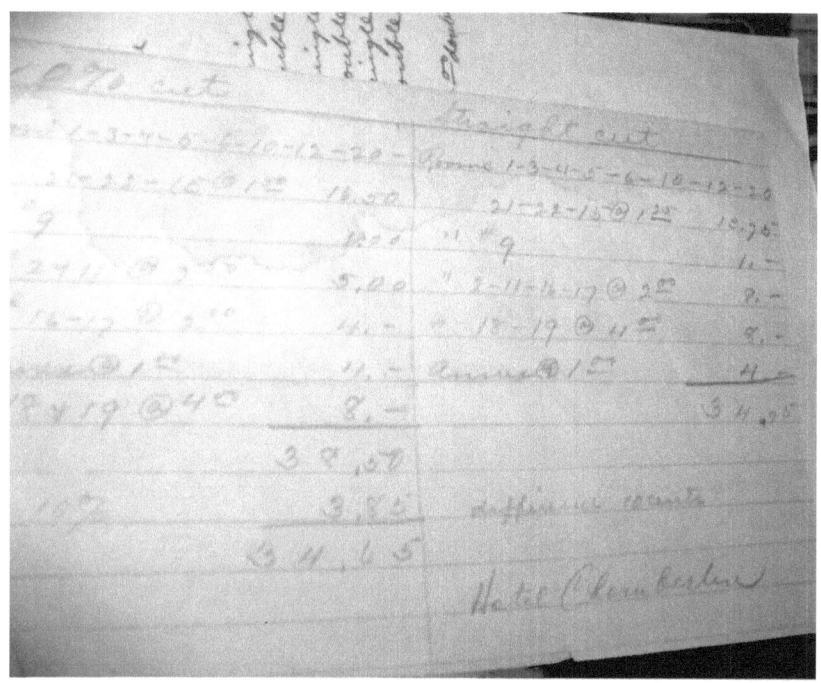

Property of Jo Jean DeHony

10% Cut

Rooms 1-3-4-5-6-10-12-

20-21-22-15 @1.50	16.50
#9	1.00
2-11 @ 2.50	5.00
16-17 2.00	4.00
Annes @ 1.00	4.00
18 & 19 @ 4.00	8.00
	———
\	38.50
10%	3.85
	———
	34.65

Straight Cut

Rooms 1-3-4-5-6-10-12-20
21-22-15 @ 1.25   13.75

#9   1.00
2-11-16-17 @ 2.00   8.00
18-19 @ 4.00   8.00
Annex @ 1.00   4.00
                                 _____
                                   34.75

Difference 10 cents

1939 Agnes retired to a Stucco house on 10th and Cody Ave

CHAPTER 16

PAWNEE HOTEL

EDITORIAL

THIS PORTION OF THE BOOK WILL CONSIST OF THE HAPPENINGS DURING THE OWNERSHIP OF THE HOTEL BY JO JEAN DEHONY

Many editorials written during my years in the hotel
This editorial was written in approximately 1985

This article could not be further from the actual history of the Cody influx of homeless and transit people if you tried. I was disturbed and shocked that you would put this type of article in the paper and make it front page. Perhaps you did not remember it being that way last year as you were too busy getting settled into your new job in a nice office, and a very nice home so it was just not something to look at or think about AT THAT TIME.

I know of sure that from the first day I purchased the Pawnee Hotel in Cody in 1974, that homeless people, and transit people have been finding their way to Cody, and getting assistance from the Social Services, the Police Department, Churches and my Hotel.

People would come into Cody with no job, very little if any money, sometimes alone, and often with a family, walking, or sleeping in their car with everything they owned to their name and would be seeking a place to sleep, eat and possibly, but not always seeking employment.

When they needed a place to stay it seemed they were always directed toward the Pawnee Hotel, and at first I could not figure this out but since I always tried to find a bed or a place for them to sleep it soon dawned on me that they were being sent where they might get help. Many times families would sleep in the front Lobby, and seek the warmth of the building, They may have slept on the floor, but they left willingly when told the guest were checking out and they would have to be out of the front lobby.

Many times I would have a bicycle with a huge pack on the back or a small cart attached to the bicycle loaded to maximum, and the person riding with very ragged cloths, and maybe some type of foot wear, maybe a car or pickup that looked like it would not see another mile, and more times than not would have all of the possessions that the occupant had to their name. It would be a big joke that I always had these cars or bikes or bedrolls in front of the hotel. Yes, they found a place to stay, even if the hotel was full, they would be able to sleep on my lawn or the patio in the back yard, and many times they could get a shower, have their dirty cloths washed and ironed, and maybe a little bite of food so they could start the next day more refreshed and then they would be on to the next town to seek shelter or perhaps some kind of handout.

I know the rates of the Hotel were very minimal in today's price range, but I would sometimes give them a room for $5.00 or $8.00, and if they did not have that, they would wash my car, or dump the garbage, maybe even help me clean my corrals, but it made them feel they were working for their room, or a glass of milk, maybe a sandwich or a piece of pie.

Social Services sometimes able to give a voucher for them to stay the night, (simply because my rates were not out of sight) and at times they would get a voucher for a meal or to have some food. Many times the Cody Cupboard or Mannahouse could and would provide some food for them, not to mention many people in Cody that helped more than anyone knew.

Don't even think that homeless people have not been a concern in the past. It was only because no one except the people and facilities that were helping them knew they were here in Cody. You might see them on the highway, in town or on the streets, looking very strange, because they did not have a car, and were not dressed like they had any cloths, unshaven, and dirty, but they were still here and they were still people that needed help.

Many people had very few cloths and we all know how bitter in the winter, and on the windy and cold days, that it can get in Cody, but they would be given a coat, a shirt, or pants, that might have been left at the Hotel because a person did not want to pack it or take it along or was simply left for someone that might be in need of this piece of clothing. They were, washed, folded and kept for someone who might be in need and be coming into Cody the next day, the next week or the next month.

No the library should not be a haven for the homeless. There could be a reasonable place for them to sleep, clean up if needed, and perhaps get a bowl of soup, but not a place for them to find a new home, and stay permanently, unless they are here honestly seeking employment, or a means to help sustain themselves.

JO JEAN THOMAS DEHONY

Don't blame this slowing national economy and the news that Wyoming is strong in the economy on homeless people and transits coming here to Cody. I fear if this type of blame spreads into our area, we will see many people lose their jobs, as an excuse to get rid of that particular employee, to cut staff, due to lack of tourist, and business. Just lower the salaries, keep all of the people working and do not let the mentality of the Washington D.C. elite spread in to our area. Don't let that happen, help everyone, and remember it's not just the transits, the homeless and the different looking stranger that needs help, any more than your neighbor, the local people that are trying everyday to pay taxes, pay utilities, pay rent, pay mortgage payments, pay car payments, put food on their table, clothe their families and just be able to live comfortably and be able to keep their heads held high in this time of Recession.

CHAPTER 17

FINDINGS AND HAPPENINGS

DAGGER SHORTLY AFTER I started the remodeling, and opened the hotel for business I hired a couple for very nice young girls to work the front desk, and to do the cleaning. We had checked in a large group of hunters from Pennsylvania, they were doctors, and hospital staff, along with a couple of hunters that owned business in Pittsburgh. I was working at Husky Oil and the Newspaper wanted to write a story on the Hotel and the New Owner. I had put this request off for many weeks, so I would have something to show for the long hours.

The day arrived, and I was at work, I had asked all of the hunters if they would mind really picking up their rooms and helping me make the hotel look nice for the reporters. After they cleaned their rooms there was nothing left in the room. I thought they had gotten mad for being asked to clean their room, and left, but when I opened the closet everything was stacked or thrown in there and it almost came tumbling out. The room sure did look nice.

The reporter arrived and took a lot of pictures, and wrote an outstanding article, but during the tour through the hotel, the desk clerk was asked to hold the Fire Hose out from the wall so they could get a good picture. When she pulled the fire hose loose from the hanger and was ready for a picture, she discovered a large dagger, in an old leather scabbard, and the handle was carved with a ugly head, the mouth wide open and teeth showing. The desk clerk called me and was so upset she did not know what to do. I hurried home and took the dagger for safe keeping only to find out what it had been hidden in that area from someone and I needed to know the reason it was stuck between the folds of the fire hose so that it could not be seen. I visited with the doctors and after looking closely at the dagger they told me the rust on the blade was from blood, and that this was a weapon used possibly to kill someone. This started a chain reaction of investigation, and one of the hunters from Chicago was a Lawyer, who was going to have me send this dagger to him as soon as he returned home. I waited for his call, and found he had a heart attack on his way home from the office, and that stopped our investigation. A business man in Cody was a friend, and advised me to contact the County Attorney that had moved away, as he felt there was an unsolved murder that happened while the County Attorney had been in Cody. This became more and more mysterious, and remained unsolved. The friend was afraid for me to have a picture or a story in the paper concerning the dagger as they were certain the dagger was a murder weapon in Cody, and that the person or persons still lived in Cody.

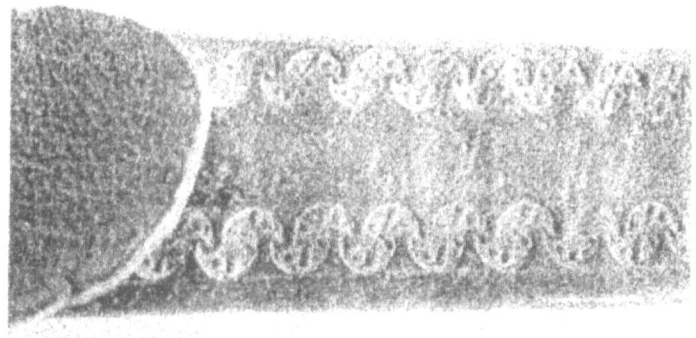

Hand-made leather sheath with hand-stamped design.
On the brass hilt on blade side, is a star with letter G in it.

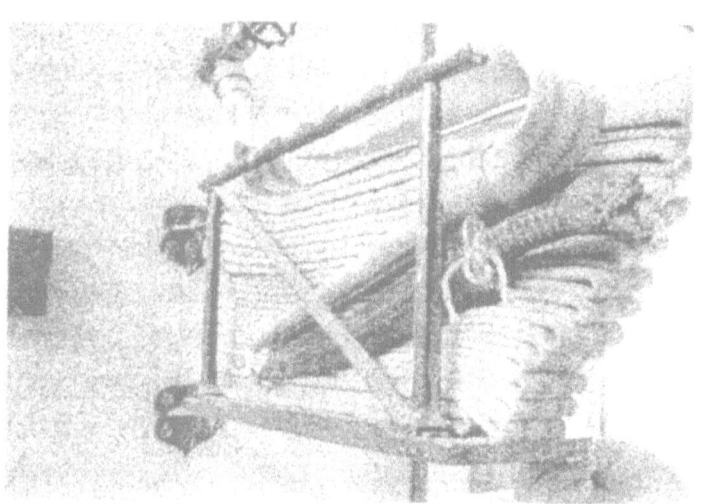

The dagger was found on the wall side of the swing-out,
folded fire hose located at the front end of the hallway, first floor.

Photos courtesy of Jo Jean DeHony

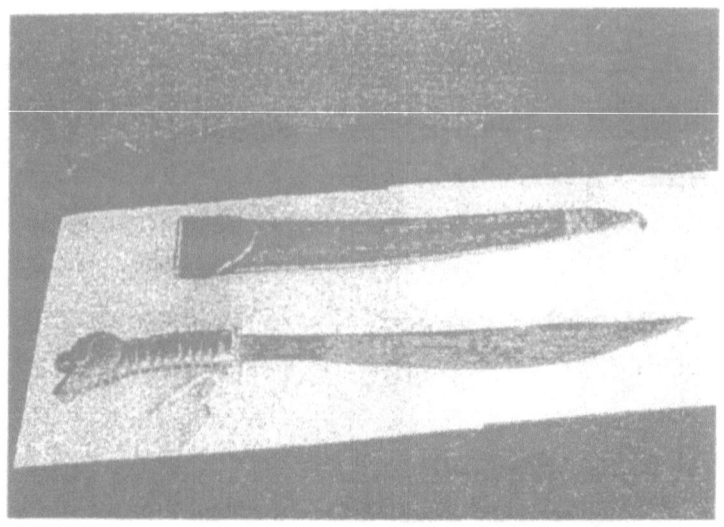

Asian dagger, possibly Philippine-made, 15 inches overall, 4 ½ inch handle
an inch thick in the widest part, with hand-made leather sheath.

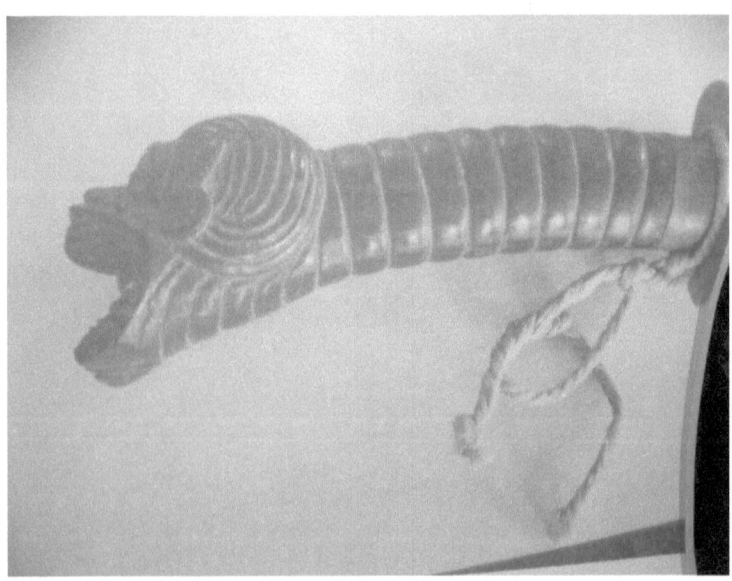

Handle, 4 ½ inches, probably rosewood, has a monkey face carved in detail:
wide-open mouth with tongue, fangs, and teeth; bands of hair
swept back to curve around ears; severed string made of hemp is
tied to base of handle; behind the face are 15 reticulated bands.

All Pictures by JoJean DeHony

FIRE HOSE The old fire hose used for the fire protection of the Chamberlin and Pawnee, was still connected to the water system. The fire hose was folded and neatly placed in a rack that held the hose along the wall in the lobby. The folds were flat, and the hose was very old, so we did not think it was a workable hose, until one day a guest decided to see if it still worked, and unfolded, it and headed out the front door, he had opened the valve. It worked and there was water everywhere. After that the large valve was turned off, the hose folded back neatly in its resting place, and was never used again, or tampered with.

PASSED OUT UNDER WOOD VINE This was one of the most horrifying experiences that turned out to be something less. I came home one early morning after being in Hyattville, and drove up in the back of the hotel, and the privacy fence to the ally was a very thick and overgrown wood vine, on the south side. I noticed a body lying under the vine, and there was no movement. I very cautiously advanced toward the body to see if I recognized it and did not, but notice it to be an elderly man. He was what seemed to be dead, I could not see any movement that you would expect if he were breathing, He was very still and I could not detect any breathing, so I touched him, and spoke to him. I asked several times are you alright, are you asleep. He moved a little and I asked him if he knew where he was. "You are sleeping in my back yard under this wood vine, and I think you should get up and go home." Again, I spoke to him. "You need to get up and go home, do you know where you are?" At that time he answered and said "Yes, I am okay, I sleep here often. Just let me rest". I repeated "You need to get up and go home." With this he did stagger to his feet and head on down the alley. I was so relieved to find he was alive, and only sleeping it off.

CHAPTER 18

INTERESTING GUEST AND BUSINESS VENTURES

KIDS IN THE ANNEX Shortly after purchasing the Hotel and remodeling it along with much work being done to remodel the Annex, the upstairs of the annex was rented to a young man and woman. They had a lot of company. The excess company led me to start getting a lot of phone calls at the office where I was employed. A call from the maid, Hannah, who had worked for the Pawnee for years before I purchased it and continued with me for many ears. She was crying and very up-set, the kids from the Annex had come to the Hotel to shower and thought it would be fun to give the maid a bad time. They started chasing her all through the hotel, and truly scared her terribly bad. She phoned and said they were crazy and she thought they were going to kill her. That prompted an immediate trip from my office to the Hotel, and I put a stop to it instantly. I instructed them it would never happen again under any circumstances, or they would lose their happy home and be asked to leave immediately. They laughed and told me they were only kidding with her, and they were sorry and apologized for scaring her, with the continued promise they would never pull a stunt like that in the future.

At the time the two kids moved out of the Annex and moved on, I went upstairs to clean the apartment and ready it for another tenant, and was surprised when I walked into the front room. They had stacked beer cans into a pyramid: A pyramid-shaped that reached to the ceiling, and was at least 8 foot across at the bottom, it was quite attractive, but . . . it took a while to get rid of all of the beer cans and was used for this structure.

DOWN ON THEIR LUCK SLEEPING IN YARD This was a common occurrence, when people would arrive in Cody, with no place to go, no money, and need to get a nights rest, they would make themselves comfortable on the lawn on the North side of the hotel, and always tried to be gone before they were discovered the next morning, but they did not know, both my mother and I were very early risers, and started out the day moving around the hotel, or in the yard. Sometimes the automatic sprinkler would come on and they would hurry out of the yard as fast as they could move.

BRUCE WITH THE HUGE KNIFE. A couple of years after the Hotel had been remodeled and rooms were being rented, I started getting a steady flow of customers, and with each, they brought a new adventure. A young gentleman, who appeared to be down on his luck, with very little, took a room there, and was a nice person that made a lot of the other guests feel very uneasy, he was always standing in the middle of their conversations, or over their shoulders when they were sitting in the lobby, and soon they lodged a complaint against him. It was really time to ask him to move on, for several reasons as well as he had a tough time getting any money to pay his rent, and would continue to act any but strange.

I asked him to move, but he came back a week later and was in a very old pickup. He was actually living in the back of this pickup. He asked me if I had any carpet and he could put in the back of the pickup and cover the homemade wooden camper type of box with canvas or a piece of carpet so he could sleep in the back. I told him to follow me and we went to a back building that I used for storage and excess carpet. We found a very large piece and I helped him carry it to the front of the hotel where the pickup was parked. The next thing was I wondered how would we cut it for the proper fit? I soon found out, as he pulled out a huge Bowie type knife, and cut down through the carpet like it was butter. At that moment, I was very uncomfortable, but never let him know how I felt. He was actually a very nice man, and very polite. I always thought he used the other personality to be different and to upset people. I never saw him after that and often wondered how he was doing, and if he was able to be comfortable and warm in his new homemade camper.

PEOPLE SLEEPING IN FRONT LOBBY Many times the yard was not the place for people to sleep, and especially if it was cold. I would awake early and go to the front to start the day in the hotel, and often would find one person or even a family sleeping in the Front Lobby, which was located, at the front of the hotel, and the entrance before coming into the Lobby where the check in desk was located. There were times when I would have a couple or a family actually take up residence in that little front area. I think the reason for this was there were radiators that lined the wall and it was warm. They were alright as long as they would get up and be gone before the paying guest started checking out. I did not like them sleeping there when people were leaving.

MAN SLEEPING ON COUCH Then sometimes one or two of the Cody's favorite would find their way into the check in lobby area, and make their bed on the couch in the lobby, this was a practice often done by a nice man by the name of "Curly", and it was just alright with me, as he would be better there than driving home, and not making it. I would wake him, tell him it was time for people to start checking out, and away he went. Honestly, when he no longer did this *"I missed him".*

NOREEN LINDERMAN, (The Outlaw Queen) a western singer with a booming voice that people loved to listen to, and dance to her music and songs. Noreen a tiny little lady with a big and booming voice. She had such volume that she did not need a mike. Noreen and her band would stay at the hotel and always chose rooms 16 and 18. This combination of the two rooms was a suite with the bath between two rooms. I always knew the next morning Noreen would be down in her robe, no makeup, and her hair was not fixed, but she would be in the kitchen the first thing when she awoke for a special cup of coffee and pleasant conversation.

BEAUTIFUL FURNITURE MADE FROM BRIDGE PLANKS During the last several years of my ownership of the Pawnee I was fortunate to enjoy a purchase I made consisting of, a beautiful table, benches, and a desk with a bench. This was crafted by a great craftsman, John Tenwald. John had crafted this set from the old bridge that had been torn out, located between the north fork and south fork and was to be replaced with a new bridge.

TWO LITTLE GIRLS LEFT IN A ROOM when their mother went out to get them something to eat, she returned with a snack, of pop and chips then immediately left again. I was unaware that she had never returned that evening. This happened later in the evening, and most everyone was asleep. She has asked me to wake them the next morning as they had to leave, but when I knocked on the door the next morning to make sure they were awake, and that I could go into do the room to make it up if they were staying, or to change it if they were leaving. I was surprised to see two little girls huddled in the bed crying. When I asked them what was wrong, they said they were hungry and their mother had not come back. I told them if they would get dressed and come downstairs, I would fix them some breakfast, thinking that I might find some information as to who they were and if they had any family. They came down, and when I asked them what they would like to eat, it was peanut butter and jelly sandwich, so that is what I fixed. While they were eating I asked if they knew anyone in Cody or close by, and found they knew the minister at a church in Greybull. I called him and he knew the grandparent. They phoned me and told me they would be in Cody as soon as they could get there, to pick up the two little girls. They arrived in about an hour, and we visited for a short while, and they left to head back to Greybull. I hoped for years that someday they would call and let me know that their mother had returned and was alright. As far as I know they never heard from their mother.

A YOUNG LADY and her family stayed several days at the Pawnee, and enjoyed Cody during their stay. This young lady was so fascinated by the large bath tubs with the claw feet. It was deep and great for a soaking bath. She asked if she could have a picture taken with her in the tub, so she could look like an old western bath. Her feet were resting on the top rounded edge with her COWGIRL BOOTS on. She had a large Cowboy hat, and she had her arms on the edge of the tub. What a great take off of the," Saturday night bath", pictured in the old western pictures.

MANY OF THE COWBOY COLLECTIBLE vendors stayed at the Pawnee. I had a great group of vendors and we became personal friends. I always said "I had the cream of the crop". They came from all over the United States to sell their special collectibles in Cody. They would come to town, and fill every room in the hotel, and always had visitors from the other motel, which we enjoyed along with our guest. It kept the hotel buzzing. I of course always had tickets to attend the collectible booths that was held for years in the Cody Auditorium, and later moved to the Recreation Center.

A LARGE SNOW STORM that hit before I found myself ready. The snow was so deep you could not get the cars out, to drive anywhere, and the only 4x4 I had was parked in back of the cars. I had to feed my horses at the other end of town so I started walking, and found the snow as over 3 ft deep, and no sidewalk, had been shoveled. The streets were still unplowed, so I made it to my little farm, fed the horses and then tackled the slow walk back to the hotel. I was out of breath by the time I made the round trip, so I had a good rest for a while before we started to clean walks.

DEEP SNOW ON SIDEWALK IN FRONT OF HOTEL which would turn to a lot of ice, if it was walked on before it was removed. But, MIKE AND JIM offered to shovel it from the front of the hotel sidewalk for $20.00. They worked all day and were dog tired when they came in and said they did not think it would be so hard to shovel, as it was becoming packed from people walking on it before it was shoveled. I took one look at them and paid them a good wage for their work. They really did deserve more than $20.00.

IT RAINED SO HARD one year while I was in the hotel, that we just watched to make sure it did not come in the door, or make certain there were no leaks where they were not suppose to be. Many of the stores in Cody were flooded. The storm drains were not handling the extra water and it was literally running in the front doors.

The Pawnee did not get flooded as it sat above the sidewalk.

Shortly after I purchased the hotel, I had the window wells all cemented in on the front of the building. This kept the water and dirt out of the basement, as well as preventing people from falling into the holes that extended out from the building onto the sidewalk at least a foot or two. When rain would build up so deep in the front of the side-walk, I had the cars back out a little from the curb, so the slush and rain could get to the storm drains.

BLACK AND WHITE TV'S When I first opened the Hotel, and had it well outfitted with new beds, bedding, carpets, furniture, and Televisions in every room. I was so proud, and I thought those 17 " Black and White Televisions was great, they had not had nice neat little TV's on hanging was brackets, and the people enjoyed them so much. Then several years later, a Lady and Man that had stayed there often, came back and brought their granddaughters. They stayed a week, and I enjoyed them all so much, but before the Lady left she said you gave my granddaughters something they had never seen. They had never watched Black and White Television, as they only knew there was colored TV's. That surprised me, but it pleased me more than I can express.

**Jo Jean and guest standing near check in desk in front lobby
Picture by Jo Jean DeHony**

PIZZAS' DELIVERED to the guest in the hotel to eat in their rooms or in the Garden north of the Hotel. The Pizza shops, always gave the guests and the Hotel special rates. Since the Pizza shops were so close to the hotel, my guest had rapid deliver time.

BREAK IN ATTEMPT on the old National cash register that I used in the hotel on the front desk for the check-ins. The cash register was large and beautiful so I felt it added to the décor of the lobby. I soon found out it was indestructible, and very hard to break into.

My laundry machine had stopped working so my mother and I took the laundry to the laundry-mat just one block from the hotel. It takes about 2 or 3 hours to do the laundry, and upon entering the front lobby I had a feeling something was wrong. I checked it out immediately and found someone had tried to break into the register with a screw driver or tool of some type in order to pry the drawer open. When that didn't work they tried going in through the paper roll area, and that did not work. I immediately called the police and the detective came down with a finger printing kit. We found the guilty party was sitting in the lobby listening and watching while we were checking the damage out. The cash register was not broken into and NO money was taken.

REUNION FOR MOTORCYCLERS A group of motorcycle riders that stayed at the Pawnee year after year, called and asked if they could have their reunion, for the group, at the Pawnee, and enjoy Cody along with spending time at their favorite bar, the great Silver Dollar Bar. I was excited to know they picked the Pawnee and that I would be able to see them all again. When they arrived, they had special treatment, with a picnic in the back yard. I fixed as many special hor de'overs. For the evening I had planned dinner at the Eagles Club, and the Auxiallary agreed to fix a nice dinner, as well as fixing the dining room up special. To top the evening off we all went upstairs and played BINGO. Can you imagine a group of motorcyclist playing Bingo. Yep they did, and it was a great evening. It turned out great, and they were and are a great group. This was their reunion in Cody at the PAWNEE HOTEL.

THIS SAME GROUP OF CYCLIST several years earlier, when they first stayed at the Pawnee, decided when they checked out of the hotel they would make a trip to the top of the hill to bid me farewell. When they arrived they all walked into the office as a group and asked to speak to me. They really gave the receptionist a scare, in their leathers, boots and all. It became quite a laughing matter when she found out they were my friends. We all went outdoors and took pictures, and bid each other good bye.

A SPECIAL RECORDING STUDIO was set up in one of the hotel rooms. I set up all of the equipment to transfer all slides, movies and many pictures to Video tapes. I set up a special hand held mike so my mother could narrate the information for the tape. She could remember the pictures, times and happenings, better than I could as they were pictures she and my father had taken along with some of my pictures. This was special, and made it complete. It was a great gift for the family at Christmas. Our mother passed away the following February.

BEDS FITTED WITH SPECIAL SHEETS I always fitted the queen beds with flowered sheets, the full beds where white, and the twins were striped. This coloring made it rapid sorting during the laundry folding. They all had the fitted bottom sheets, so the beds were always very neat, smooth with good fitting sheets. This type of bedding also gave each room a special and different appearance, not just the one color fits all.

CLOTHSLINE IN BACK YARD that had been put there for the purpose of drying the sheets, or cloths. This line was there when I purchased the hotel and I was not going to remove it as I enjoy the fresh smell of the sheets and towels from hanging in the air. Many of the guests also enjoyed having it there. They would dry their cloths after the river floats, the fishing trips, the rains that hit them on motorcycles or just to get the freshness of the breeze and sun while their cloths were hanging outdoors.

PICTURES, BRONZES, BOOKS this is only a few items that I had in the hotel as gifts from the guests and the people that I was fortunate to meet and get to know. Other items that I had just arranged or sitting around in the Lobby was a beautiful old SLOT MACHINE for display only, Antique juke box, Old books, records, pictures, historical items, several old hotel registers from 1917 to 1924, with many interesting stories told about several people whose names we found. One lady looking through a register found her father's name. She told me he used to boot leg from Red Lodge to Cody and stay in the hotel, and she found his name in the room next to the room the Judge was staying in. She made the remark, "what better place to stay, other than next to the Judge".

Not to mention numerous old boots, that always intrigued people. The guests had a lot of questions as to why I had so many pair of boots in the Lobby. I always made up a story, that any time a cowboy came to the hotel, he had to leave his books in the lobby, before he went up to his room, I didn't want them sleeping with their boots on, and many had forgotten their boots when they left the next morning. We would have a great laugh over this made up story.

BUFFALO BILL MUSEUM recommended the Pawnee to the people that came to Cody for their classes. They would get a very special rate, and stay for several days or several weeks at a time. I would always enjoy hearing what they were working on, or the special items they were studying.

THE CODY HOSPITAL also made arrangements for special rates. In return they would recommend the Pawnee to families, or individuals who had someone in the hospital. They would usually have several days stay waiting for their family to be ready to go home. The Pawnee was a place to stay for one night or great rates for an extended time. The Pawnee was homey, comfortable and everyone felt very welcome.

LARGE LAUNDRY ROOM IN ONE PART OF THE ANNEX. When I started to remodel the Annex I took the part that had been a garage for Mrs. Chamberlin's Old Essex vehicle, and a sleeping room for a person that she let stay there and help around the yard. I moved the Large Milnor wash machine, and a huge dryer into the area after enlarging the door, putting a very nice cement floor, with a water drain, and fixed it up with a heater, for warmth. This area was used for the daily chore of doing the laundry that was most often performed by Jo Jean and Erma. The annex was a building in the back and very close to the entry of the Pawnee Hotel.

A STACK OF METAL SIGNS with the imprint "Pawnee Hotel, sensible, central rates" these sign must have been printed when the name was first changed from Hotel Chamberlin to Pawnee Hotel, They were a collectable item. The gentleman that had them gave me several of the signs. What a treasure. I appreciated them so much.

SCULPTING, PAINTING, KNITTING, The comfortable atmosphere of the Hotel was a perfect place to construct what—ever hobby or craft my mother and I could come up with. My mother had many beautiful items she had knitted or crocheted, and they were available for people to purchase. They were a special hand-made gift or keepsake. I would knit and sculpt, as well as a couple of paintings. I guess between the work in the hotel we always found time for those specials items.

TRANSOMS ABOVE DOORS for air needed to be closed to prevent too much lighting and hallway noise, but they were perfect for the nice breeze from the window being open and the transom drawing the fresh air through the room. When the air conditioners were on it would work in reverse, and draw the air conditioner air through the room and out the window. Some—times the transums were not meant to be open. One evening the noise was so loud coming from a woman and man making love, that the whole up upstairs hall was lighted up, with every door opened while the guests were laughing and listening. I knocked on the couple's door and told them to breathe a little more quietly of course the audience was not happy that the show was over.

BICYCLES, SKIS, AND OUTSIDE SPORTS EQUIPMENT was to be left outside of the rooms or in the front lobby. Many people had to be talked to firmly and they did not want to leave them. I would explain how much extra cleaning they created if they were not clean. One instance was cute and I got a chuckle out of it when I looked up the stairs, a group of young people were leaning over the banister, and as a group said "GOOD NIGHT MOM".

ARCHOLOGIST AND GROUP WITH KERBY SEIBER FROM SWITZERLAND This group worked the digs in Shell, Wyoming, looking for dinosaur bones, and Kerby made certain they all stayed at the Pawnee, when they arrived in Cody, also when they came to town for groceries or items they needed for the Dig. They always stayed with us, when they left. When we could get together, I would take my family or friends out to the digs to see what they were doing. It was so interesting to watch them work, to see what they did while digging, and getting their bones ready for shipment. It is a true art to gently dig the bones, dust them, and handle them so carefully.

DECORATION AT HALLOWEEN AND COSTUMES. Each year we would decorate the hotel for Halloween, and sit around waiting for the guest in our costumes. Sometimes we were bolder and would dress up and go all over town. One year two of the girls ladies that worked for me in the hotel and I dressed up as an old hillbilly couple and had one of the girls on a lease as out pet cat. We went to every open business we could find, and to our surprise, no one knew us, but we had a great time. The people that worked in the hotel were always such great sports and enjoyed having a big laugh.

MAKING ICE CREAM, CHURNING IT BY HAND We were having a nice picnic on the patio at the Hotel with some special guest, and decided it was time to make homemade ice cream, and churn our own, but I had a couple of the older guys that said there was no way they would churn the ice cream, my remark was, "if you want any to eat you will", they did, and while some were churning the others were out trying to get a new lawn mower started. It took about 5 guys to try to figure it out and finally some woman asked what the little black bulb on the side was for? It was to prime the mower, and GUESS WHAT? It worked and one pull on the rope and the mower started. We ate, had homemade ice cream and a great visit with a lot of great friends.

JO JEAN THOMAS DEHONY

How many does it take to start a lawn mower?
Picture by Jo Jean DeHony

AIRPORT PICKUP FOR THE HOTEL was a special I did for any out of town guest, that did not want to rent a car, but just a ride to the hotel. They stayed for a day or week, shopped in Cody, went to the museum, art shops, and enjoyed their visit, then back to the airport to fly home.

TAKING PEOPLE TO HOSPITAL, AND DOCTORS, This was a regular thing for me to do. Many of the guest were without cars, were locals, or just some one that needed a ride, and I felt it was a thing I could do for someone that needed help. I enjoyed being able to help people when they needed it. A lot of people did not have family, and they would put my name on the hospital register as the one to be notified if they were released or needed anything.

SNEAK AROUND AND STEALING FROM OWNER keys were made to fit the office door. When I hired a middle aged man to work in the hotel, I thought I was doing the right thing until I found him in my private living quarters, or in my room when I came home from work one afternoon early. I asked him, "what were you doing in my room" he replied " I was in the laundry room". That was a blatan lie, as I had seen him coming out of my room. Later, I caught him going into the office that was keyed only for my mother and I to enter. I came home one evening and found a key left in the lock on the door, and checked it out. I immediately made a trip to Gambles to see if they had made the key, which they had. He had found a key and had a duplicate made and was using it to enter the office, my living quarters, and stealing money from my bed room, out of my purse if it was left in the living room and be gone for a short time. In questioning him, and bringing it to a head, he admitted stealing over $4,000.00 from me over a few months, and was using it to gamble with at the club next door to the hotel. I made a movie recording of his admitting what he had done, along with insisting he write me an admission of his theft. He did this willingly as he knew where he could end up. I did give the recording and the letter to the police department to be used for his arrest.

When they called me and told me they would be by to pick him up I decided to let him go and make him work it off, with very little pay, to live on with the balance being used to pay back the money he had stolen. It took a long time, but he did get it paid back, and then I terminated his employment. He worked for a camp ground, and one evening he was driving back from Pahaska, after having a few drinks, he ran off the road into the river, and was killed. I did feel very bad about his death. I also knew he had a tool box I had given him to carry his money collection in, but when I asked the investigating officers if they had found it, they had and were holding it. I knew he had a large collection of dollars, as he still owed the coin company money, as I would get bills for the coins he had ordered. I never did see the money, and was unable to send it back to the company he was buying the coins from. It was a sad ending for him, but it was his ending, and I found none of his family had anything to do with him. He was buried in the Cody Cemetary, with a few of his friends attending the service.

NO CLOTHS ON GUEST AFTER SHOWERING Having a public shower and bathroom in the hallway between all rooms, gave the guest the opportunity to shower and go back to their room. One Guest did that exact thing, and only had his towel to wrap around him, which covered him very sufficiently. But . . . a young lady living in one of the center rooms, walked out of her room at the same time, and actually went into hysteria, screaming and crying. I had to intervene and told her to never act like that again, that the man was perfectly okay, and needed to get to his room, after using the public shower, and he was showing her no threat.

GAY COUPLES A NEW EXPERIENCE When gay couples became more open. I was certainly not aware of this, and was more than surprised when it was not long until there were a few times when a couple of guest would come to check into the hotel. I found they were a couple, two persons of the same gender and not being aware of this type of actions, I always insisted on giving them a room with two beds, and they would often say, "oh no, one bed will be just fine". One day not so long after this happened a couple of times, it was all explained to me. SURPRISE!!

DRUNKS ON 4TH OF July LOCKED OUT OF ROOM. On the Fourth of July it was a very common thing with many of our guests. I was very patient with them as most of them were very gracious, and good in the hotel, but now and then some things would erupt, and I WOULD HAVE TO GET INVOLVED. One evening the wife came home early, as she had just had enough of the parades, drinking, bars, crowds, so she was already in the room and most assuredly already asleep, when her husband came back to the hotel, and quietly went up stairs and tried to get in the room, knocking quietly, and whispering "let me in". Well she had, had it and locked him out and would not let him in the room. It did get a little loud, so I went upstairs, and visited with both. Since then, and years later it was well talked about, and laughed about, when I visit with this couple. No harm was done, but it was a very funny situation.

FECES IN BATHTUB—I had adjoining rooms 16 and 18 that used the same bathroom, bath area. One morning a man from 18 came down to the front desk and told me I needed to see the terrible mess in the tub in the adjoining bathroom. He said the tub was full of water, and looked like someone had used it for a toilet, and it was full of FECES. I asked him why he did not drain it out, and he said "I ain't going to put my hand in that". I want upstairs to see what the problem was, and to my surprise it was terrible. I got a cloths hanger, straightened it out and pulled the plug out of the tub, and let the water out. I was very upset thinking that one of my guest could make such a mess. After I cleaned it up, disinfected everything, I made my way to his room, and was going to have him leave the hotel, but he was gone, and was apparently moving out, he knew what he had done. He apparently came in late, drunk, and had messed his cloths and took them off and put them in the tub to wash. This was only one thing in a lot that happened, such as the next comment.

URINE IN THE CARPET In the same set of rooms 16 and 18 with the adjoining bathroom, and #24 also used the same bathroom. Each room also had their own sink. I had rented 18 to a little older man, that was a steady guest, of the hotel if he did not want to go to his own place. Sometimes he would stay for a week or more. I had rented #24 to a couple of young boys. I was unaware of the problem that was going on between the boys and the man, but found they would not let him go to the bathroom, so over a period of two or three days, he had to go, and just wet on the floor, which was carpeted. When I found this out, I kicked the boys out with a firm scolding, and had to have the man move to his apartment. I started to clean his room, but it was impossible, as the carpet stunk, and was wet and stained. I pulled up the carpet to find the urine had gone into the wood flooring, and saturated it with the smell of urine and was wet. My mother and I scrubbed, used purex, used pine sol, and soap, opened all the windows, and scrubbed it again and again and let it dry until it finally lost the odor, then varnished the floor, and re-carpeted it after we were sure it was clean. Another room was back in service after a month of lost income.

FECES ALL OVER A ROOM #18 again was the victim of a mess. My mother and I had gotten home from Hawaii, where we had gone to vacation, and found the desk clerk had rented #18 to a man that spent a great deal of time in the bars. One morning he made his way through the hotel taking everything he could pick up, registration cards, pens, and items out the desk, then on down the hall into the kitchen where he picked up an arm load of gloves. On to the refrigerator, and got a large container of Poi, that we had brought home from Hawaii. He ran out the back door, and threw everything in the dumpster. Seeing him do this my mother and the long time cleaning lady went to the dumpster to get the items out. As these items from the front office was needed to operate the hotel. They were leaning into the dumpster with one holding the others legs so she would not fall in. The man that owned Yellowstone gift saw them and laughed out loud. He teased them about picking the dumpster. The next day they were getting ready to clean rooms and when they got to #18 where this man stayed, the one that had taken the poi, they were horrified, and came out gagging, saying they could not go into the room. He had literally messed all over the room, on the walls, the sink, the floor. It was a terrible mess, so once again we tore everything out of the room, cleaned, disinfected, and re-did the floor, the walls, and re-carpeted it again. It seemed we had something happen often, and knew it was part of owning and operating a hotel. But it was a whole lot easier to laugh than cry.

BLACK WOMAN MAID I rented a room to a couple one evening, they were dark skinned, and at that time in Cody, this was not seen often. I gave them a room, and the next morning I had a gentleman come down stairs, and asked if the Maid had said anything about his wallet and money. I inquired what he meant, at which time he related to me that the maid had come into his room very early and said she was going to clean the room, but would come back. I was shocked as I did not have a colored maid. She had stolen his wallet and money from the top of the dresser. They had already checked out, so I could not question them. We started looking around as I just could not believe this had happened in the Hotel. We searched everywhere, and about a week later I was moving a couch to clean behind. The couch sat just below the stairs for some time and this was where they had dropped the wallet from the stairs-way from the second floor to the lobby. The wallet was empty she had taken the contents, and knew she could hide the wallet until she was a safe distance from the hotel.

POT IN # 21 When I rented this room I smelled a strange smell coming from it, when the guest was smoking. Not knowing anything about marijuana, I thought that was what it was. When I went in to clean the room I noticed a large flat box on the bed, filled with leaves and some seeds, and called the police. I thought he was smoking pot. They came over and took some samples to the station to test, and we found it was alfalfa. He was smoking alfalfa, and not sure if he knew the difference. We were all surprised and he was in no trouble.

FOOT MESSAGER It was very late one evening and I felt it was not unusual for late guest check-ins, but always used caution, and always had my mother there to watch from the back room if I had a problem. I had the bell ring about 2 A.M. and got up to check this guest in. He was slightly inebriated, and decided I need a foot massage, to make me sleep better. I told him no and to go to his room so I could get back to my sleep. Next thing I knew he was on his knees at the side of the desk and was insisting on a foot massage. This made me very uncomfortable, and I then insisted he go to his room or leave. He went to his room. I didn't get my foot message.

THE APPLE BLOSSOM AND LILACS WERE FRAGRANT AND BEAUTIFUL the flowering crab trees, and the lilac bushes were so colorful, fragrant, and beautiful. There were two trees and several bushes in the yard so they could be admired by the guest on the north side of the hotel, as well as the passer-byes, driving on the west and north streets or walking past the hotel.

SAMOAN CHASED A COUPLE OF YOUNG KIDS DOWN THE ALLEY INTO THE HOTEL A young couple staying at the hotel had gone for a walk down town and stopped in one of the bars to check things out, when they happened to make a comment about this very large Samoan, and he apparently, did not like what they said and started after them, chasing them down the alley toward the hotel. They flew in the front door and upstairs slamming the door to the front lobby behind them, and the Samoan tried to come through it without opening it, breaking the small panes and shattering glass down the hall and past the front desk. I ran out and yelled at him, asking him what the devil he thought he was doing. He took off down the alley and disappeared. Not to say this was a several hour job cleaning up the glass, calling the police department, and trying to find the Samoan to talk to about the damage. Nothing was done as restitution, so I cleaned up the mess and had the glass panes replaced. I did have a nice talk with the young couple. They were checking out, and they were still afraid of him.

TITLES OF VECHILES WAS NOT UNCOMMON When some of the guest would fail to pay their rent, and this would be after they were several months late, I would request the title to their vehicle until they paid their rent, and if they did not they would lose their vehicle. It would be sold for the back rent. It might sound like a harsh treatment, but it was not, I was always letting people stay and stay until they owed far too much, and they just figured they did not need to pay it.

AFTER 31 YEARS IN THE HOTEL YOU WOULD THINK I KNEW EVERY CORNER, When I was moving after all of those years I happened to be in the basement and the electricity went out, it was pitch black, and I was totally turned around and lost. I could not find my way out, and finally one of the people upstairs heard me and opened the door at the top stairs. They had a flash light. That was truly scary and a very strange feeling. I actually ended up in the old coal room, and for the life of me I could not figure out the wall I was standing in front of and could not find the door out of the room.

VERSITILE FIREPLACE IN THE LOBBY OF THE HOTEL. A great fireplace, that I understood from several people that had been in the hotel, was wonderful and used a great deal, but I decided it would be too much work and too messy to burn wood, so I had it changed to electric, that did not heat, so I changed it to a gas burning fireplace, and it was beautiful, but really did not give out a lot of heat, so it was changed once again back to the original wood burning fireplace. I was not the best fire starter when trying to start a fire in a fireplace and of course this smoked up the lobby and part of the upstairs often. A lesson I had to learn. Get a good draw, and make sure I did not let the smoke get out into the interior of the hotel. Once I learned how to adjust the damper, and all of the tricks, it was great, and what a nice warmth in the Ole Pawnee Hotel.

A GREAT BAKER OF EXCELLENT PASTRY When I hired a lady to help in the housekeeping I soon learned she was a great pastry maker, and cook. She worked there for a few months until I noticed I was buying way too many baking pans, and a great deal of spoons, bowls, measuring cups, and anything she could find in the store across the street that she might want to use for her baking. When the purchases were out of reason, we decided it was time for her to try another location. But her cheese cakes were exceptionally delicious.

MICHELLE. A GREAT JOKESTER, AND SOMEONE WE COULD HAVE A LOT TO FUN WITH when she went on a week-long trip so one of the guest and I decided to pull a trick on her. When she came home the hotel was locked with all of the lights out, the door had a large sign on it saying "due to lack of help, I am forced to close the hotel" When she got to the door and read the sign, we were quietly hiding in the porch next to the front door watching everything. She looked very startled and was talking to herself under her breath, and hurried up stairs. She was all over the hotel looking for me. When she was about to start crying or getting very upset, we turned on the lights and asked her what was wrong. She was so upset she just stood there and cried and laughed. We have talked about this so often since then and always find it so funny the way she acted.

DISPLAY CASES IN LOBBY FILLED WITH MEMORABILIA Items I had found in the up-stair secret room, including dance books from Mrs. Chamberlin, the original Irma hotel menu, old glasses, cuff links, small flags, some small sparkler fire crackers. I also filled them with special small gifts and items given to me by many of the guests. They were my treasures.

MOTHER, SISTER AND BROTHER IN LAW ALWAYS THERE WITH LOADS OF FOOD If I planned a big picnic in the yard for a special celebration, we always had loads of food, lots to eat, and a lot of company to eat it. These special foods were prepared by my sister Gay, my mother and me. It seemed Gay and Jerry was always there when I needed help or an extra hand. Meats, salads and desserts, all that a person could want. UMMM Delicious. We always had a great group of people, and several musicians, such as Ken Owens and Judy Almeda, two good friends and guest at the Pawnee Hotel, they played their guitars and beautiful voices entertained for a great Fourth of July celebration. The 4th of July picnics was always in the back yard on the north side of the hotel in a nicely groomed garden area. We had a large number of people from the hotel along with some people who would just stop in thinking it was a park. One great 4th we had some relatives moving from Dakota to Tennessee, they came by after I called and made our acquaintance. It seemed everyone enjoyed it so much. It was an excellent spot to sit and relax on a hot summer day. One 4th of July we roasted a whole 260 pound pig on a spit, all night, that kept two guys up making sure it kept turning, and did not tear off the foil wrap when it would catch on the barbeque grill. This pig fed over 50 people, not to say how much each person took home. I know my deep freeze was full of pork for months. What fun and something to always remember.

BAG PIPERS FROM BILLINGS came to Cody each year on the 3rd and 4th of July and participated in the Parade. After the parade I asked them to join a group of people on the patio and lawn on the North side of the Pawnee for a picnic. They joined us and entertained the guest with several songs. What beautiful music. During their stay they tried to show my young 6 year old nephew, Greg how to blow a bag pipe, but it was not long before he found he did not have enough air to make more than a squawk. "I think they take more air than he was big". They are a little hard to blow.

POODLES—TOY AND STANDARD POODLES that I raised for several years, were one of the best pleasures I had. The large standards were kept in a nice large pen with a heated dog house. We had a litter of standards and a litter of toys every year, and they were sold to many great owners, all over the United States. The standards, for hunting dogs, guard dogs, personal pets, and also used to work on a cattle ranch. The toys were just sweet and little and were purchased by some very special people. Of course I kept a toy from each litter, with the excuse that I wanted to see what the litter would turn out like. I loved the cute little guys and gals so much. I kept 2 of the standards, and what beautiful and friendly dogs. I traveled to Arizona to sell standards poodles that I raised and bronzes that I purchased from several artists for the purpose of resale.

MAN TO BUY HOTEL WHEN I WAS CLEANING DOG PEN I was out in the back yard cleaning and washing down the large dog kennel, when a young man drove up and asked me if the place was for sale, I said sure come on over and help me clean the dog pen. I thought he was joking until the next day when he called again and asked if he could come by and visit with me concerning the purchasing of the hotel. I was shocked, and pleased, but did not want to sell the hotel, as I was always so pleased with things that happened, and how much success I felt I had in my own little business. That was only one offer of many after that, and finally I did make the big decision and sold the hotel.

CODY: This man came into the Hotel to stay, as he was down on his luck, no money, he had gone to Social Services, and needed a room. He soon had a female partner, and I found he was drinking a bottle of hard liquor, every day or two. One day when he came down to pay his rent, he opened his wallet and I could not believe what I saw. He had more 100 dollar bills and bills of all denominations in that wallet. More money than I had ever seen in anyone's wallet. I was in shock. I asked him, why he was on Social Services when he had so much money. He laughed and said he not only got help from Cody, but also Powell, and that was only the half of it, he had 200 head of cattle in Montana, and had money coming in from oil royalties. I just looked at him, and told him I was ashamed of him or anyone that would take advantage of the help from the Social Service, when so many people needed it so badly. He just stood there in front of me and laughed as if it was a huge joke.

MANY AUTHORS OF BOOKS STAYED AT THE HOTEL, It was always such an honor to be mentioned in their books, and it was always very complimentary. A lady stayed at the hotel while interning at the museum. She would walk past the Irma hotel each day, and when she finished her book she had mentioned the Pawnee and the Irma, and several very interesting things in Cody. A young man stayed at the hotel for a few days while he was traveling across country, and found it very interesting and made nice comments in his book, then several years later this same young man brought his son, and the son was writing his book of poems for kids while his father was involved in another book. The authors were so nice and presented me with a complimentary copy of their books. How interesting, and this was only a few people, plus the Pawnee was mentioned in all European travel guides, and North American guides for travelers, they said it was a favorite place to stay as it was homey, inexpensive and very clean and comfortable. This was a very high compliment to me, and to my staff and the hotel. Thank you.

HAM BONE IN STOOL The upstairs apartment in the Annex was rented to Jim. Before he had been there long, he was taking up all of the new and heavy furniture he could buy, A huge TV, large couch, big bed, the apartment was very small, a kitchen, small bath, and a bedroom, but he was making a nice living area and it was his home. One day he said the stool stopped working, we plunged, we worked on it for two or three days. Then the straw that broke the camel's back was when Mike who was down stairs, and who was a best friend of the person directly upstairs above his kitchen, told him he had to get the stool fixed, as every time he sat down to eat, the water from the flush of the stool was coming through the ceiling and onto his table and getting into the food he was eating. He thought it was really a bother when his cereal was soggy every morning. But one day I just decided instead of constantly trying to fix it I pulled the stool, took it down stairs, put in a new one, took the old one out on the lawn to see if I could find something wrong with it. I decided to find out what in the world caused the blockage. GUESS WHAT? He had fixed ham and beans a week or so before and they were turning bad, so he just flushed them down the stool. There was a huge ham bone in the pot of beans and it did not flush out of the neck in the stool. Believe me he did get an ear full, and to this day when I joke with him, I remind him of his HAM AND BEANS. Jim lived there for a long while after that incident. This was only one of the many times I said "it is easier to laugh, than to cry".

VITAMIN SHOP: I sold a very good vitamin and food supplement for a long period of time. This started shortly after the Beauty Salon was opened, and continued when I leased the salon and put the vitamins in the back part of the Beauty area. I would give demonstrations on the dried food and had a good customer base. They are still available, but I do not work at it like I did at that time.

BOOK STORE For a very short time after I closed the beauty shop in the front of the hotel, and before I remodeled it into 4 very nice rooms, I put in a book store, as I had boxes of books. I sold a lot of very collectible books, and had a lot of paperbacks. Before long I began trading books, and found that I could not spend concentrated time in the book store, so decided to close it and take a lot of the books to the Salvation Army store.

FISH SHOP My mother and I decided we wanted a fish store, and sell all fresh water fish. It became very successful and had customers from very early morning until late into the night. One day my mother called and was very upset as a water fall was flooding into the fish shop just as you walked through the door. It was coming from upstairs. I had to laugh when it was over. My mother was taking a customer into the shop at that moment, and I joked that I bet she thought it was the most effective way to enter a fish shop that she had ever seen.

I rushed home and found the man that was renting the apartment overflowing with water. I rushed into the room to find 2 very large knives lying on the table as I entered the front door, this made me very apprehensive. At that time he was telling me he was being electrocuted when he sat in a chair against the east wall. This being impossible, but to make him feel better, I called the electrician, the cops, the plumber, and warned them as they arrived that he had the knives, and was not acting normal. They went into the apartment and checked everything, and took him out eventually taking him to jail. In checking around I found before coming to Cody he had lived in Sheridan. I immediately called the place he had lived in Sheridan, and found that he turned a hose on and let it run in the gutter for hours, and just simply loved to watch water run. Then I was told they let him out of jail and a week later the Irma Hotel called and said they thought they had my guest there. He was supposedly been sent to Sheridan to the VA Hospital, but instead he was just let out of jail, and checked into the Irma. He was barricaded in his room with the mattress and tables against the door and no one could get into the room.

We found in checking on several things that he also had taken boards and nailed all the windows and doors closed in his apartment in Sheridan. Further checking I found from the guest in my hotel that were in the room backing up to his room that only a couple of days earlier he had stacked the mattress against the adjoining wall and that he was hitting the wall and yelling most of the night trying to keep people out of his room. This was a impossibility as it was a solid brick wall and no one could have gotten through or into his room. He was soon taken to the hospital in Sheridan. Apparently they knew him and he had been there before. This was where he needed to be in order to keep him safe.

JO JEAN THOMAS DEHONY

MUD IN HOTEL BY HUNTERS, The first year this group of hunters stayed at the hotel, they did not realize it was not only my hotel but also my home. They came in that evening after hunting all day, and everything was muddy. They laid their muddy guns and scabbards on the furniture, and their boots were thick with mud. When they tracked it into the hotel and started up stairs to their rooms, I stopped them and asked them if they would do that in their own home. They took off their boots, and I made sure they had newspapers laid outside their room door to put the muddy boots. I guess it worked as the next morning all of their shoes were sitting outside their door, and they did not put them on until they got downstairs and ready to leave. Great group of guys.

HUNTERS There have been so many hunters, and outfitters from all over the United States stayed at the Pawnee, and each was very special in their personalities. John, One of the hunters who later started cooking for the Outfitter, brought his wife, Diane to stay in the Hotel for several years and we became lasting friends. The Porter Outfitter, would book his hunters in the hotel, this became a yearly occurrence, and I grew to know each and every hunter, and their families. We have stayed in contact even after their hunting in Wyoming faded. We would have great dinners, and cookouts. At one time I had a group of doctors and friends, that were Italian, I do like Italian food, so they agreed to fix me a 5 course dinner, if I would in turn fix them a wild game dinner, with a multiple of different wild game species. We did this! We made an exchange and both meals were very large dinners, fit for a king and the large living room used as living quarters was turned into a dining room. We fed at least 30 people each dinner. What a great time, and how delicious.

MOTORCYCLE RIDERS A few years after I had remodeled the hotel, motorcycle riders became popular, and the one name that was talked about with some fear, and some inquisitiveness was the Hell's Angels. I was apprehensive about having them in the hotel, and really, was not ready for a large group of motorcycles. My mother and I took a drive one evening to check the fill up on the motels, and to drive up toward the Buffalo Bill Reservoir and a directing a very large group of motorcycles to leave. I made the remark "Boy that will be out luck to have them at the hotel". Never thinking anymore about this incident, we headed home, and as we turned left onto 12th street, in front of the hotel sat 25 motor cycles and their riders. I was not sure what to do, but I played it very cool, drove around back, where I parked, went into the hotel and up front into the lobby, unlocked the door, and was greeted with a very large group of motor cycle riders, in their leather jackets and blue jeans, and was asking if I had room for the group. I did not, but decided we would just make something work so I started with telling them how many rooms were available, and the only thing left was the large front porch upstairs, that had windows surrounding the room on two sides. No shower, but they could use the public shower. We started moving roll-away cots into the room, and making up the beds, and that room actually held about 10 or 11 men, then we put 4 into another large room next to the porch. Then continued the room search and bunking them together with beds and roll away cots, until they all had a place to sleep. What a great group of guys and gals and they came back years and years after that. The Pawnee Hotel was their home and the Silver Dollar Bar was their club room. As we continue there will be more mention of the great times we had in the hotel with the motor cycle riders from all over the United States and Foreign Countries.

YARD TORN UP FOR MOTORCYCLES The year the City of Cody decided to host the Motor Cycle Rally, was the year I met some of the best and most polite people that have stayed in the Pawnee. I truly had the hotel booked full and could not take any more guest. Then a surprise came through the front door and his name was DON. He told me that they had been booked into the Holiday, and when they arrived they did not have their rooms and they wanted to send them up the North Fork about 25 miles, on 10 miles of construction. We had been having rain for several days and the roads were a muddy mess especially for motorcycles, as they do not do well in mud or soft dirt. They needed a place to stay. They all had camp trailers pulled behind the motorcycles and they had very good means to set up tents, and sleep outdoors, so we talked a while and I had a large yard, with a lot of lawn space, but I also had a lot of beautiful flowers.

Don and I went into the yard and surveyed the situation. I told them I could dig out a row of the flowers so they could get their trailers and set up camp on the North lawn, as well as the lawn close to the hotel. We proceeded and they moved in. The next morning while at my office I received a call from Don and he told me he had rounded up about 10 more couples that were with their group and needed a place to stay so he would just move them in and make room. I said "OK". When I arrived home from work I had a complete village of tents and camps of every color and every level and what a great bunch of people. I only had one public bathroom in the hotel, and at that time I also had a nice Hot tub room with flowers, and the whole set up, with another bathroom. They used them both, and it was nothing to see the Hot Tub room running over with people. But to add to the problems it rained every day they were here, so no one wanted to be outdoors for long. They made it all work, and I was made an honorary member of their club. Just one year later I made a trip to California and was taken on one of their pie runs into the mountains. One owned a motor cycle shop, so I was decked out with a helmet, and everything I needed to safely ride behind one of the large motorcycles and found first-hand what a wonderful time they had when they went on their rides. I was given the helmet and other items as a very nice gift before I left for home. Many years after that some of the old group and some new members always found their way back to the Pawnee, and after that day they all had a room with a private bath, and found many very nice eating establishments in and around the Cody area, as they were not camping out after the first trip.

You are probably asking if all of the motor cycle riders were always so nice, and I will tell you they were not, at least for a while. There would be times when people had ridden days, and double, and it was hard on them as I soon found out with a group from a second Rally they had in Cody. The group of riders arrived, and they were checking in with laughter and great enthusiasm after their long ride, until one lady started on her husband and on me. She was registered into one of the best rooms on the main floor, and that was when I became a little disgruntled. She started in that she could be staying and the 7-Ks with their friends, instead of a hotel in down town Cody. I politely told her to pack up her bags and the cycle and go to the 7-K's and to not come back, I also asked her husband if he had had to put up with that mouth all the way from their home to Cody? It was at that very instant she changed and asked if they could go ahead and stay, I then told her if she could be happy, and keep her mouth shut it would be fine with me. They checked in, and in about 10 minutes she came out to ask if she could have a drink in her room, and I made a joke and asked her when she was going to invite me. We both laughed, and from then on every time she saw me whether across the street, or in the hotel, she would yell Hi and wave she became very friendly and a very nice person. SHE WAS JUST TIRED!

MARINE BAND Each year on the 3rd and 4th and most often the 5th of July, the Cody Parade Committee had a lot of out of town entertainment, and always some that was really special. The Marine Band had been brought to Cody for several years, and there were always over 30 Marines that traveled with this portion of the Marine Band. I was fortunate enough to be the Hotel to get the Lodging contract and enjoyed it a great deal. My mother and I would make a trip to Billings to pick up at least 20 or more rental roll-aways and prepare them for the band members. I would get two of the largest areas and put at least 8 to 10 cots to each room, and then use the balance of the regular rooms for the rest of the Band members.

This was always interesting and a great time as the Marines were the greatest and enjoyed their stay, they enjoyed the Pawnee Hotel and the town of Cody.

LARGE FAMILY IN LIVING ROOM The second year the hotel was open for business, I had a very large group of people I believe three families, that could not find lodging anywhere in Cody, so I told them they could all stay in the large living room I had, but they would need to sleep on roll aways. They did and they were happy to have a bed. I had to stay out of my living quarters that night and the next day until they left. They were a very nice group and appreciated the lodging and beds to sleep on.

CUTTING UP DEER IN BACK One year the hunters from the Back East were lucky on their first day of the hunt and had about 15 deer, to be cut up and processed, with no place to have it done at that time, as we did not know of any individual that processed game, so that put 15 deer in my living room (there was no furniture or anything in there except the old original linoleum). They had been dressed and skinned, so I took on the job of cutting and wrapping. WHAT A JOB! That was a one-time deal, believe me.

BIRD MAN This man stayed in the hotel every year, and each year he registered under a different name, and I would remind him that I did not forget easily, and to use the right name. This young man had many superstitions, he always went up the stairs, and would sit outside of his room for 30 minutes or more. I am not sure what the reason was for that, but any time he left the hotel, he always went out the back door. One day he was sitting outside a room, of a very nice young Cowboy (Harry) that stayed at the hotel on a weekly or monthly basis. When the cowboy came out of his room, he asked the man why he was sitting there, and was told that he was waiting for the birds to leave the room. Well, it did not take long for the Cowboy to hi-tail it downstairs and ask me was in the world was going on, and he did not want that man in front of his door. I immediately went upstairs, and visited with him, then he slowly walked on to his own room.

Now for the real surprise, about 3 days later I was in a downstairs room that had a back door, that we would leave open often in order to freshen up the room and the hotel, and guess what, I walked into the room, and there were two birds in there that had flown in from the back yard. What a joke that turned into when I told the Cowboy. "Guess what we do have birds in the rooms". "There was nothing wrong with that man outside of your door a couple of days ago". Once again we had some good laughs, but I was afore warned.

COWBOYS One of the greatest groups of people that wandered into the hotel many nights, were the Cowboys, from in and around Cody, from ranch workers, to rodeo hands, and from visitors to entertainers. They were always

JO JEAN THOMAS DEHONY

welcome and always had a lot to talk about, with stories that were welcome, but a whole lot of BS went along with those stories.

This led to a great editorial when the hotel was sold, wondering "Where will the Cowboys go". I cannot find a copy of this editorial, and wish I could as I would include it in this area.

I was very pleased to have the rodeo announcer and his wife stay with us, for several years, when he would journey to Cody to announce the Cody Night Rodeo.

STAR WARS MOVIE Another regular guest always stayed in the hotel and insisted on room #16, as it had a channel that he could get Star Wars on. He enjoyed these movies more than anything on the TV. He could not get them on any other TV. HE ALWAYS GOT THAT ROOM, even if sometimes we would have to change reservations around.

MONSTER LAKE SOUTH OF CODY Many times I had a great fisherman that would come to stay at the PAWNEE HOTEL when they came to Cody. He would bring his friends or his daughter. They came to fish the Monster Lake. They enjoyed that fishing lake more than any other area in Cody. When they called for reservations they always requested fans in their rooms, and blankets on the windows, the fans for the sound that they were so used to and the blankets on the windows so they were assured of complete dark with no lights from the streets lighting. They slept as late as they wanted, or went to bed as early as they wanted and had total darkness with the humming sound of the fans, this assured them a nice rest, so they could go out and tackle the fishing.

LATE NIGHTS IN THE BARS Being the hotel owner, it seemed a regular thing to help people to their rooms after spending too much time in the bars across the ally from the hotel. They would slip on the ice in the alley, or just have a hard time getting to their room. I would help them upstairs, and make sure they at least laid down on the bed. I did not want them falling back down the stairs. Several guests, and to name a few, Lee, several Jims', Warren, several Bills, Austin, Terry, Danny, a couple guys named Mike, they were all special in their own way.

GREAT ARTIST WITH BIC BALL POINT PEN This young man could actually sketch anything, and it was beautiful. All with a ball point pen. He stayed at the hotel several times, and one night he was staying in the annex. When he came home he was afraid, and had to leave immediately as there was a bunch after him. He was scared, and I told him to just get as far away as he could and hoped he would not be hurt. I never saw him again.

GUN AT THE THROAT OF GUEST One late evening I heard a noise in the back yard, and found a group of men that had been to the bar too long was teasing my big dog that was in the kennel, and the man that was renting the apartment in the back was there trying to get them to stop teasing the dog. He was shoving them away, and a woman jumped on his back. Not knowing if it was a man or woman he turned around and knocked her off his back, and at that time the group of men grabbed him, bent him back over a car and put a gun in his throat under his chin. I ran out and still in my robe, I yelled at them to stop, and that I would call the cops before they did something to be sorry for. I called the cops and they each got arrested and spent the night or longer in jail. They were all telling me I knew them and not to call the cop, but I told them they deserved what they got. I felt that they were very dangerous with the gun, and probably lucky they did not pull the trigger in the condition they were in. The woman got her dues. My renter was safe, and the dog was not teased again.

FIGHTS IN ANNEX The annex in the back of the hotel was at one time a barn owned my Mrs. Chamberlin. I felt this building would make an excellent building for apartments, and therefore, remodeled and rented out two larger apartments, one up stairs and one down stairs. I did have many interesting guests in the annex from two elderly gentlemen, that lived there before I purchased the hotel, later two young kids, that decorated the upstairs room with beer cans, one a young girl that ended up with multiple cats, (she was not suppose to have), couples in upstairs and down stairs, and We had some big fights in the annex between the couples and the police were called in numerous times, but only if it got too bad, like one woman getting tossed through the screen door, and breaking some glass, but all in all they all proved to be interesting, and each in their own way, was good people.

I did have an elderly rancher staying in the downstairs that passed away in one of the apartments in the annex. I went out to wake him to see how he was doing and was very upset to see he was off the bed, and had tipped over the lamp and had the bedding pulled off the bed with him. I called 911 and they arrived immediately. He was pronounced dead, which was a sad situation as he was such a wonderful person.

DUCKS I had a number of Rail Roaders, that stayed each night at the hotel, and they were a nice group of workers. One evening they told me they were going to bring me a duck. I expected a grown duck, and one that I could turn into the large lawn on the north side of the hotel.

I immediately got busy building a wire cage so it could be loose to eat on the lawn, but not get away. To my surprise when the duck arrived, it was a baby about a day or two old, and it looked very small in this large wire pen, I had spend all day building. I took the duck and babied it along and it grew, and grew fast, I had people passing by and always noticing the duck, and wanting to feed it. I even had full heads of lettuce being bought and brought to the Hotel to feed the Duck. It was not long until I had two more baby ducks, and as they grew, I knew I must find a good home for them, so I checked around and found a great place north of Cody, with ponds, and a lot of forage, and other ducks for them to join, I was given permission to take them to this new home and turn them loose. My mother and I made a trip to the new home, and made sure they found a new home, with lots of ducks.

I am sure your have be wondering, as you read, if we had ghost? The following section will tell you a little about OUR GHOST.

CHAPTER 19

GHOST OF THE PAWNEE HOTEL

GHOST REPORTS ROOM 17 AND 9 This was a surprise to me to find the hotel had Ghost, but it was also a thrill, and created a lot of inquisitive thoughts. The first appearance that I was aware she made was about 12 to 15 years after I purchased the hotel and had completed a great deal of remodeling. I had remembered the rooms and the one this very un-intrusive and silent lady appeared in was #17, (this was the numbering I had made on the rooms after starting the remodeling)

This was a big room at the top of the stairs. When my guest checked in and went upstairs to his room, he opened the door to enter, and encountered this lady sitting on the bed.

He turned around and came down stairs and told me I had rented the room to another guest. I knew this was not possible and asked him about the appearance and who it was? What they were doing?

He said she was sitting on the bed in a long blue dress as if she was waiting for someone or she was just sitting there thinking. When he entered the room she just got to her feet and left the room.

This was the last I heard about her until a young man checked into the room I had numbered 25. He did not mention his seeing this lady, but his sister who was in another room came down the next day and mentioned to me that her brother had seen this lady and was afraid to tell me for fear I would laugh at him. I did not get to visit with him about this lady he saw in his room, as he left as soon as they came downstairs.

Another time a young lady told me that her friend had seen a ghost in room 23, but he would not talk about it to anyone, as he felt they would think he was strange or just seeing things. That's about all I heard of that time, but wish I could have learned more from the young man.

The Lady of the Hotel (I will call her this as it seems a better description than the Ghost of the Hotel). This lady returned several times during my ownership of the Pawnee Hotel.

I believe she actually belonged to the time of the Hotel Chamberlin, prior to the name change, but she came back several times to view the changes and to approve of what was being done to rebuild her Hotel and make certain she thought it was the way she wanted it to be The hotel had stayed the same for many years, with nothing being done, or very little being done to improve it, and was being rented with much of the same furniture, and the same way it was when she operated it.

I heard nothing about the lady in the blue dress, until several years later when I remodeled the down stairs, and made 4 rooms in the area where I had previously had a beauty shop, a fish store, a book store, and settled on making 4 new rooms.

I checked a couple into the room I numbered 9 which was just to the south immediately after you enter the main Lobby. This room was in the area, where Dr. Chamberlin had his dentist office. The next morning the lady came out and asked me if I knew I had ghost in the hotel. I told her "no, I never realized it, but please tell me about what you saw". She told me had seen a nice looking woman in a blue dress visiting with a gentleman, and she called him Clyde, she was not certain about the last name but thought it was Johnson. She said they were standing in the corner next to the door. I did not think too much more about this until her husband came out and asked me the same question. I thought they had talked to each other and was joking with me, but they assured me they had not discussed this, and they had both seen and related the same incident.

Years later while I was doing more research and reading Mrs. Chamberlin's editorials, and writings, she mentioned a Clyde Johnson, who came to the hotel often and was from Sheridan. was a very active member, a lay reader for the Christian Science Church, and I can only assume this was the person they saw and believe it had to be Mrs. Chamberlin, they saw visiting with him.

Seeing Ghost, or visitors from the past is a hard thing for a lot of people to tell you about, thinking they will be made fun of. It is becoming more talked about now, and a lot of people find it very interesting.

I personally never had the pleasure of seeing this lady, but I do believe my guest did see her and that she was making her appearance at a particular time and in a particular area to check out what was being done and giving her approval or perhaps she had other reasons, but I do believe this lady was checking on her hotel and perhaps meeting with a person, who was very important in her life that she felt close to, and at this time while I am writing this, I hope she has found peace, and approves of what I did with "Her Hotel".

When you own a Hotel that is in the middle of a small western town, and surrounded by restaurants, bars, and many other businesses you will never run out of experiences and things to talk about.

I will group the next items and only hit the highlights. Such as the delivery trucks for the bars and restaurants would come in during the night, and leave the trucks running while they unloaded. The diesel would come into the windows in the hotel on the second floor, and about gas guests. I constantly fought this and needed the assistance of the city cops to help me. One bright early morning about 4 A.M., a truck was running in the alley just below a window, and next to the hotel where the diesel could pour into the windows. I ran out in my robe, and had not taken time to comb my hair, but grabbed a broom to tap on the cab window to get his attention.

The driver was out and in the restaurant making his deliver, and when he heard me he came around the corner of the truck and I guess my appearance and having a broom, startled him. Not sure what he thought I was, but soon found out I was a very upset hotel owner, and wanted my guests to get a good night rest. "Shut the truck off."

It seemed every car or truck that parked in the alley behind the bars, would back out when they were leaving to go home, and sure enough they would hit the hotel, drop into a window well and need pulled out, and it was not long until I thought they were going to knock the hotel down or put a big hole in it. I called the city and they installed a large railing with 4 inch pipes all along the side of the hotel in the alley. This put a stop to hitting the hotel, and no more cars in the window wells but it did cause a lot of broken tail lights.

MAN MAD AND SITTING ON BLOCKS of cement in the back of the hotel in the city parking lot, staring at me as he had just been asked to leave the hotel for causing a disturbance. I walked over to him, and told him his staring was not going to upset me and if he didn't leave, I would call the cops and have him removed. He left.

There were times I would have to replace a window, as people would toss a small rock up to get someone's attention, and oops it would break a window, or they might think an innocent shot with a B B gun would get a guest attention, not thinking it would break a window. Or at least put a hole in it.

It was not an unusual thing for me to climb onto the roof of the hotel through a small escape door from the old laundry room, and onto the top of the hotel to clean out the water gutters, as they would fill up with leaves and dirt, or to fix a belt on the large air conditioners, or may be change a fuse. Scrape the ice off the roof it there was a problem. It was a flat roof and really not a dangerous place to be, but I did not enjoy cleaning the rain gutters, as I had to lean too far over the edge, and I am not a person that enjoys heights.

My guests in the hotel were such an array of personalities. I had a wonderful group of people from the Cowboy Collectibles, the Gun shows, the Car Shows, Trade Shows, Motor Cyclist. Single people, married couples, cowboys, ranchers, patients for the acupuncture doctors, and hospital, families, and it seemed they all became friends.

We had a large group of Hells Angle's, and did not know it until the next morning when they came down in all their leathers and silver on the belts. They were working on a Bike in the back of the hotel, and I received a call for a person. I walked out to see if he was in the group, and they would not give me an answer. So I gathered they were not interested in who was calling.

One large group of girls was traveling across the country, and made reservations at the hotel. They were sales persons that worked for different companies, would reserve a room each time they came to Cody. The biggest surprise was when (one who left several dresser drawers full of Jewelry). We found it and kept it until they contacted us and was coming back to pick up their possessions.

BAILING GUEST OUT OF JAIL was not an unusual thing, as I would get calls from some of the guests that I knew well, and they stayed at the hotel often. They might spend too much time in the bar, or have a little too much to drink, just to get picked up. They would call and tell me what they wanted to sell me if I would bail them out. They said they would pay me as soon as they could. I never doubted them, and when they got out I would take them back to the hotel, they would stay the evening rather than try to drive or get home. I received money, guns, and other items to hold until they could redeem them. Some would redeem and others just left them so I would find a way to sell them, or trade them to someone in order to get my money back for the bail money. I never made a bad move on doing this for these people that I knew and considered friends.

It was not long that the law changed and the people picked up had to stay overnight. I could not bail them out that night, but as soon as I could the next morning, I would take their bail to the jail and get them out.

One morning early a regular guest walked through the door, and did not look too good. I asked him, "where have you been?", he said, "in jail, I got picked up for drunken walkin". I joked with him, as I did not believe him, but he soon convinced me.

When I opened the hotel and was working in the lobby, a neighbor who lived about 1 block away walked into the hotel, and looked terrible. When I asked him "what had happened"? He told me he had been in jail, I ask "my golly what for?" To my surprise he told me he had gotten so tired of the loud music from the patio at the Silver Dollar, that he had gone over and with an ax chopped all of the wires to their instruments and speakers in half, and was arrested. I was surprised, but guess he had his reasons. I told him I was glad he was alright and to go home and get some rest.

I know hotel and motels will allow dogs, or have no pets allowed, but I would get many types of pets. I had a great couple that stayed at the hotel monthly or more often, and they had a beautiful BIRD, their PET, they would bring each time. But soon they had a beautiful little daughter, and they would bring her with them each time. When they moved to another state I really missed their regular overnight stays. He would sell at the 7 D's ranch when he came to town.

LOCKS ON FRONT LOBBY DOOR AND KEY FOR EACH ROOM, were used on each hotel tag. The lobby door lock would be changed often to keep the past guest from just walking in and taking a key. I kept a key box behind the check—in desk, which made the room keys easy to get for check-ins that had pre-paid or for late arrivals if they had a reservation, and I was not available when they arrived. But sometimes they were too easy to get by someone not having a room, if they were able to get into the front lobby with a friend or another guest. I did watch that, and would check the register each morning when we were preparing to clean rooms. If a key was missing I would know it and check to see who was trying for a free room.

FIRE IN HOTEL ON 4TH OF JULY, I WAS FISHING, at the lake on the north fork, and what a surprise, I drove down Sheridan Avenue coming home, and turned left onto 12th street to find fire trucks, and a lot of vehicles with flashing lights. I thought boy wouldn't that be something if I had a fire in the hotel, and guess what I did, one of the air conditioners, had a belt burn and put out a lot of smoke that was blown into the lobby and appeared to be a fire. But that was not much different than in the winter time when I would try to start the fire place, and never get the draft right, in order to make the smoke rise, and it would fill the lobby and some of the upstairs with smoke. That caused some excitement.

THIS INCIDENT WAS A HUGE SURPRISE and a little shocking but a lady I had known for a lot of years was parked in front of the hotel and needed help getting into her car. I offered my help and when I was trying to lift her and her legs into the car, I was shocked and not sure just what to do as I had PULLED HER LEG OFF. I did not know she had been in an accident and had an artificial leg. But she laughed, made some joke about it and before it was over we were all laughing and got her in the car so they could go home.

JO JEAN THOMAS DEHONY

FIREFIGHTERS GROUP was staying at the hotel the night when a big house fire just one block away, broke out. They offered their help, and stayed close in case they were needed, but the Cody Fire Department arrived, and handled it in a very good and usual manner. This group of firefighters were from several areas and were all traveling together.

A large group of firefighters from back East
spending a couple of nights at the Pawnee Hotel
Picture by Jo Jean DeHony

A very nice young man was staying at the hotel and the Buffalo Bill Bar was next door, where they could go to play pool. He decided to use that for an evening of entertainment before he left the next day, but when he came back he only had a collar around his neck and he had been beaten up so badly that he had to stay several days. We worked with him fixed him meals to eat and tried to doctor him back to get well so he could travel. Never sure why he was beaten up on.

I had travelers with all types of transportation stay at the hotel, such as a bicycle loaded with everything the man owned, and he would travel across the United States. He stayed at the Pawnee many times over the years. He would always pick up a few odd jobs while in Cody, and became a known figure. He was a good worker, and minded his own business.

This was only one on a bicycle, the one that I felt was worthy of a picture was a bicycle with a very heavy pack and little trailer loaded with everything a person could possibly want to live with. He did not have a travel trailer.

YOUNG GIRL ON SMALL MOPED, TRAVELING ACROSS THE UNITED STATES AND CANADA. I was concerned about her traveling alone, but she seemed to think it was just a joy to go where she wanted when she wanted, and all by herself. She pulled into the parking space in front of the Pawnee, checked in and asked if she could park her Moped in the alley behind the large brick building south of the Hotel. I told her I did not think they would mind and it was quite secure.

We had so many things happening at the hotel. When my mother and I took a trip to Hawaii, I asked a personal friend if she would be willing to stay and take care of the Hotel. She seemed delighted to watch the hotel while we were gone. She enjoyed the guest so much. One of the Rail Roaders that stayed in the hotel when they were on the Cody run enjoyed teasing her. When he came in one evening and found MARY DAVIS SLEEPING ON COUCH UNDER NEWSPAPER. He was joking with her when he told her that he had a bum friend that used to sleep under newspapers on the park benches. She said it kept her warm, and she did not want to get up and get a blanket. Mary was a great person and a very good friend of the family.

We had a lot of fun BABY SITTING A RACCOON that belonged to my Sister and Brother in law. He would crawl up on the top of your head and brush your hair around like he was trying to make a bed. Sorta gave you a thrill, as you were not sure how far he would go. I had a group of motorcyclist staying at the hotel that evening, and they had a lot of fun with him.

Decorating the hotel for the Holidays that I had time for and the main one was especially CHRISTMAS, the lobby was decorated, a beautiful tree sat in the corner, next to the large fire place, and when it came time for opening presents we would all sit in the lobby have hot cider and enjoy the evening. Many times my mother and I had guests that joined us.

THE OLD FURNACE CAUSED SOME EXCITEMENT a few times. If the furnace was not filled and checked on a regular basis you could have a lot of problems. I will never forget the evening the basement filled with steam, and the BOILER heat gauge was so high that I was afraid it could blow up. I immediately made it to the basement and drained it off. I learned a lot the first few years I owned the hotel.

It was not long until I needed to purchase a new furnace. IT TOOK TWO, INSTEAD OF ONE to supply the same amount of hot water, but they worked great. It did not change the fact that the RADIATORS would built up steam, if the water was too high in the lines, they would steam and water would leak out of the valve on the end of the radiator and they would need to be bled off. As soon as you released air you would get the heat from the Radiator. If there was air built up in the lines, you could hear the radiators banging and keeping you awake, I would drain them off and then it was a peaceful nights rest. I doubt that anyone that owns an older hotel never gets a full-night's sleep.

LANDSCAPING THE YARD ON THE NORTH SIDE OF THE HOTEL, was a project for many years, with flowers, trees, a new patio, and then decided it would be nice to have a Spa Room in the ground floor of the Annex. This way the motor-cyclist and several guest were able to use it and enjoy it. I came home one day and walked into the spa room to find the room with was filled with ice. A water break upstairs had leaked a lot of water, and being so cold that evening the water froze on the tub, on the walls, and about 3 inches thick on the floor. It really made a large mess so I took the tub, the flooring, and pictures out of the room and remodeled it into another room. It ended up I never got to use my own Spa room more than maybe 3 times. This ended the Spa that my mother and I had looked forward to so much, just using the nice warm water with the messaging jets so we could relax after a long hard day in the hotel.

When people would come into Cody, and filled to the overflow, with all motels, hotels, along with many homes filled I would start putting people anywhere we could to let them get a good night's sleep. One evening I had 4 beds with men traveling across the country, all SLEEPING IN THE BEAUTY SHOP. They did have to get up early and get out as the beauty shop opened for business at 8 A.M.

I had a young man that stayed in the hotel for several months, and believe me we had a lot of incidents with him:

One evening when I had rented to this young man, he was acting very strange, and was sitting in the lobby. He jumped up and broke the side off the leather couch, and went up stairs, and broke into his room by busting the door and look. I went upstairs and ordered him to leave, we got into a rounder, he hit me a good one on the side of my face, so I grabbed him by his long hair and was hanging on when I yelled at the desk clerk to call the cops.

There was a gentleman that was a cop from Illinois, and he ran up stairs to help me, only to get into a real scuffle with this young man. When the cops arrived, they were going round and round upstairs, and I noticed the cops had an item in his hand, and thought it was a microphone to record what was happening. It was mace, and when they went upstairs, I yelled at them to not spray the man with the black hair, he was helping, but they just sprayed both, and the mace was all over the hotel. The young man had super strength, as he was drinking and was on drugs, He hit a cop and knocked his glasses off and down stairs. They finally got him down and handcuffed him to take him to their cop car. The cops told me to get wet towels for everyone. We were all sitting around with towels.

One of the guest a young lady from back East, came into the hotel and I asked her to go to her room as we were having a problem. She said no, I've never seen this much excitement in New York. She was excited and thrilled to see all of this going on. She sat down and grabbed a wet towel.

This same young man had stayed in the hotel several times, and I never knew what to expect from him One morning I entered his room to make it up and he was sitting on the bed, cross legged, under a small perfectly made priamid hanging from the ceiling, he said "Shsss, I am meditating". I left the room and let him finish, and a little later that day I told him to take it down from the ceiling.

I would tell you if he stayed upstairs, he literally floated down, as I don't think he ever walked down. He was so quiet. One morning, he was coming down stairs and the whole side of his head was bloody. He was very confused, and I asked him what had happened, and told him he better not get my pillows bloody. He told me he had been robbed and knocked out and slid down the side of the bank. The outside of the building was rough and really scraped his face. The bank was located at the end of the ally from the hotel. We found sometime that day that his buddy had hit him and robbed him as he wanted some money. A short time later they were friends again.

He would receive packages, and one day I noticed person after person going upstairs to his room. I went up and knocked on the door, told him to open the door, as I felt something was wrong. When he opened the door, I know there were over 25 kids in the very small room. They grabbed something from the table, ran down stairs, and scattered it in the alley. I could only see some small black seeds and not sure what it was, but after so many things happening, I told him I felt he needed to find another place to live.

AN OLD REFRIGERATOR operated with gas was in the basement and it was so heavy that 4 men could not lift it up the stairs to remove it, when I sold the hotel. When we all started to pull and lift it out of the basement it fell back and trapped a couple of men that was on the bottom end, so I just left it.

RAILROADERS AND FIRE EXTINGUISHER A big joke took place in room #28. WHEN a group from one crew decided to wake one of their friend up with a fire extinguisher, not knowing what a terrible mess it would make. The next morning when the ladies went into the room to make up the room it looked like a large power puff. The foam from the extinguisher was all over the walls, the bed, the dresser, cloths you name it. It took a long time to get it cleaned and washed off the walls the furniture, out of the carpet. I was not happy with them and informed them that they would have to pay for the clean-up and the mess. They each chipped in to pay for the clean-up.

TIMBER JACK AND LARGE PICTURE In the front lobby, it was as tall as the ceiling, and about 5 ft wide. This picture was of Timber Jack, his dog Tuffy and his great Horse. Timber Jack always stopped at the hotel to say Hi, and we enjoyed his stories, and his visits. He would talk about his life and his experiences, and perhaps we can give you some insite into Joe's life.

He appeared to be a living mountain man just stepping out of pages written about, a dozen other mountain men over the years. Grizzled? Yes. Old? Knowledgeable? Yes. And you could defiantly recognize him by his cloths, his hat, his glove, and his great dog Tuffy.

Timber Jack Joe was born in Gillette, Wyoming, on March 8, but I do not now what year. He was born to Isaac. The family raised sheep for their main source of income and food. At the age of six Joe was given charge of a large band of sheep to watch over on summer range. This task occupied Joe every summer until 1934 when depression and drought made things difficult for anyone who lived on very little.

Joe had been a heavy equipment operator, road builder, timber man, coal miner. In the late 50's he began running a trap line in those beautiful mountains, he loved so much.

It was during this time that Joe began to care for, and train, injured birds and animals, the most memorable being an eagle with a broken wing. The eagle and Joe were inseparable until the government forced him to release the bird. And since the eagle could not fly due to the useless wing, martens killed it very quickly. For a while Joe added a young fox to his menagerie, along with his dog, Tuffy. Tuffy and Joe have been inseparable for over 18 years.

Timber Jack Joe had been featured in National television, and had a program of his own on Channel 9 in Casper. He would mingle with school children to teach them basic survival skills, and other areas of his expertise.

Movies have asked for the services of Timber Jack Joe. He has been sculpted, painted, and written about. He is a member of nearly every Indian tribe in Montana and Wyoming. And he is a 'blood relative' of Jeremiah Johnson, thanks to the friendship with a nephew of Jim Bridger.

Timber Jack Joe Lynde, and Tuffy, have been featured in parades all over the west. Rodeos, county and state fairs, dedication ceremonies, judging panels, Pow Wows. Timber Jack Joe is a member of the Missouri and Wyoming Divisions of the National pony Express Association.

CHAPTER 20

JUST ANOTHER NIGHT OF EXCITEMENT IN THE HOTEL

I STILL LAUGH AS an incident that happened to my niece Cindy, when I asked her if she would take care of the hotel while my mother and I went to Billings, and she seemed very willing. About 9 or 10 P. M. I received a call from her and she wondered if these Railroaders were crazy. She had just been to the beauty shop and had her hair fixed and when she got to the hotel, she checked in the guest for the evening and soon received a phone call for a railroader in one of the rooms. Remember the rooms all had transoms above the door that opened to circulate the air, when she knocked on the door to give the message from the phone call through the transom. The railroader thought it was another railroader giving him a bad time, and he threw water through the transom all over him, but got Cindy instead. Talk about being as "mad as a wet hen". She was.

I called them and told them they owned her a huge apology. I asked what they were thinking, to do such a thing, and found they had been heckling this particular railroader all day, and he was fed up.

They apologized to Cindy and I think it made things okay, but secretly I still laugh about it.

BAD GUYS UPSTAIRS. These men were giving my mother a bad time. I was working in apartment on Rumsey, when my mother came over and said she was having trouble and needed help. My mother was telling me what happened and I would not accept anyone being disrespectful or unkind to my mother. I immediately went to the hotel. I entered their room and had already lost my temper. I explained to them I would not tolerate their actions, and did not want them as guest. They were ordered out, told to pack their bags and not come back. They left immediately.

When I started the remodeling process, I found some small stairs, entering the large living room, from the back stairway. They were not safe, and did not look right for the remodeling I was doing. I wanted to transform the small square stairs to a very large rounded stair way with a nice landing. I had a young man, Jim, that helped me with many of the projects I dreamed up in the hotel. One of which was the rounded stairs, which we worked on for a while, and when we finished they looked very nice, and were still there when I sold the hotel.

I had the excitement of having some people in the hotel that must have found it a place to stay and be away from places where they could be found, by people they did not want to see. Many times a young man would come to the hotel to rent a room by the week or month, and ask to not allow anyone in his room or bother him unless he gave me the name of the person he wanted to see. If they lived in a trailer or apartment, they could be gotten to easily, and the hotel had a front entrance and desk, were the people had to go through the desk clerk to visit the guest.

I had a couple of ESCAPEES from an institute, that I noticed had been there before and was picked up, so I called the police and told them that I had sent them to the bar to get a list of names for employment and they would be back shortly. One did come back and grabbed the bags of cloths, they were carrying and took them out the front door and started scattering them all over the street. They were picked up and found they had escaped again.

This was traumatic, but was slightly amusing when it was all over, I had a man in a room that had been staying there for a couple of weeks, and was calling a friend and acting strange. The person he had been talking to called me and asked me to check on him as he was worried about him after his last conversation. I did and found he had put dead bolt locks on the door and I could not get in, but I kept talking to him, and he finally opened the deadbolt. When I got into the room, he was hanging from a cloths rack, with a robe belt around his neck. He was still alive and the only reason he was alive, is the belt stretched, and he was able to stretch it to the point he was on his knees. He had tipped over his coffee pot, and the table next to the door and directly under the cloths rack. We got him down and laid him on the floor called 911 and the police, and all he could say was that his throat hurt. I told him I wonder why, he had the belt tied around and was handing from the cloths rack. They took him to the hospital, and his family came to get him. Thanks to the fact that robes are made of a material that stretches.

I had a few young people staying in the duplex. The source of heat was from a floor furnace, located in a wooden man made fireplace, and was in the room on the main floor. It actually heated the entire apartment. They had placed their rubber overshoes on the heater to dry them, and they caught on fire. The duplex was a smoked up mess, the walls, curtains and everything were a black fuzzy decor. There was a beautiful large United States flag hanging in the hall way going up stairs, it was black and looked like velvet. It did require a cleaning company to come in to clean, and repaint. It took the cleaning company about 1 month to clean it and try to get the smoke smell out, to be repainted, and redo the ceilings and walls where the fire department had chopped holes in them to see if they could find the source of the fire.

I ran out of rooms and let a traveler stay in his TENT on my lawn, but told him the SPRINKLERS would come on around 6 A.M. so be sure and try to get up before then to keep from getting wet. The next morning I went out to check the yard, I noticed a big group of Motorcyclist was standing on the side walk laughing and found him dodging in and out of his tent trying to get out between the water spray. I had to laugh but I did go over and shut down the system so he could get out and put his tent in an area to dry off.

One of my special guest, and I will name him: Jim Johnson has been a regular off and on guest for over 30 years. He first stayed in the hotel in a room, he made a comment that he probably stayed in every room in the hotel from time to time. He had a brother Gordon that was often with him at first. They stayed in a small apartment in the hotel, next an apartment in the back of the hotel, later moved to a small farm I had, and lived in a house at the farm then when Jim moved this last time he is now staying in my apartment in town.

Never let it be said that during the first few years of ownership of the Pawnee Hotel that I did not have a lot of CITY HALL DISAGREEMENTS, consisting of the Raw Water, the sidewalks, the lighting, the signage, the insulation sprayed on the exterior covering on the Old Hotel, and a lot of items that I guess I have forgotten. It seemed that the Mayor, the City Clerk and I always seemed to get things settled. They were very dramatic at the time. I look back and think just how hard it is to own a business. There is always something new that you have to be aware of in order to comply. Just know what you want and be firm in your request.

I sold the hotel in 2005, to a very nice couple by the name of Ev and Susan Diehl, who have renamed the Pawnee Hotel to Chamberlin Inn. They have completely renovated the buildings, and the property which is now surrounded by a beautiful brick fence, that encloses the property for the privacy of their guest. I look forward to this hotel that sits in the center of down town Cody to continue for many years into the future.

Bub and I have moved 6 miles from down town to a small farm on the outskirts of Cody. We have wonderful neighbors that are always here when you need them. The animals; horses, llamas, goats, chickens, dogs, cats, and a never ending supply of deer, as well as on a few occasions, cougars, fox, coyotes, skunks, raccoons and a multiple of different types of birds. It is a good life, but I

JO JEAN THOMAS DEHONY

still miss the Hotel and seeing the wonderful friends I met. People from all over the United States and many Foreign Countries and realize what a wonderful opportunity I had during those years with the challenges, the variety of new things that I encountered and being able to become involved in the lives of so many people. This is only a portion of the happenings while I owned the Pawnee, but there is not time and room to put them in this book. I will just keep them in my memories.

This concludes my book, and I hope you have enjoyed—WHAT LED TO 'LIFE IN THE HOTEL", HOTEL HISTORY.

Jo Jean

SOURCES

ORIGINAL WRITINGS BY AGNES CHAMBERLIN

CODY ENTERPRISE NEWS ARTICLES

PICTURES AND TEXT FROM WYOMING TALES AND TRAILS

PICTURES BY JO JEAN DEHONY

INFORMATION GATHERED BY ESTHER JOHANSSON MURRAY AND INFORMATION FROM JO JEAN DEHONY AND HOTEL REGISTERS

BOOK OF AGNES CHAMBERLIN WRITTEN BY ESTHER JOHANSSON MURRAY

PICTURES FROM PARK COUNTY ARCHIVES

INFORMATION FROM CODY HISTORICAL INFORMATION IN LIBRARY

INFORMATION FROM GUEST, AND LOCAL PEOPLE WITH MEMORIES

AUTOBIOGRAPHY

JO JEAN THOMAS DeHony the second of three girls raised by loving parents in a small town at the foot of the Big Horn Mountains. (Hyattville, Wyoming}. Population near 100 people.

They owned a grocery store, and a small farm, where they had a number of animals and lived close to, an abundance of wild animals. Jo Jean was a person to imagine things and always dreamed up ideas and thinking of something new. Art, painting, and sculpting, remodeling and working with her horses.

Jo Jean wrote a few short stories for the enjoyment of the family and friends. After schooling, she worked for an Oil Company (Humble Oil) in Worland, Wyoming. After Humble Oil closed, Jo Jean moved to Cody, and worked 25 years for Husky Oil. The last years at the Husky Oil, she was determined to open a beauty shop, which lead to the purchase of the Old Pawnee Hotel, that was in a state of disrepair located in down town Cody 1 block from the main street,. She started remodeling and being inquisitive, she started research. Finding old letters, as well as stories and pictures given to her. During the ownership of the Pawnee so many things happened that Jo Jean insisted she needed to write a book. In 2010 she started a book dated from 1897 to 2005, at which time she sold the Hotel. At that time her ideas became a reality, with the completion of this book the Life in the Hotel, Hotel History.

www.ingramcontent.com/pod-product-compliance
Lightning Source LLC
Chambersburg PA
CBHW030923180526
45163CB00002B/443